THE NEW DEISM

THE NEW DEISM

Divine Intervention and the Human Condition

Richard Sturch

ST. MARTIN'S PRESS
NEW YORK

© Richard Sturch, 1990

All rights reserved. For information, write:
Scholarly and Reference Division,
St. Martin's Press, Inc., 175 Fifth Avenue, New York, NY 10010

First published in the United States of America in 1990

Printed and bound in the UK by
Antony Rowe Ltd., Chippenham, Wilts.

ISBN 0-312-04793-2

Library of Congress Cataloguing-in-Publication Data

Sturch, Richard.
　The new deism: divine and human activity in the world / Richard Sturch.
　p. cm.
　Includes bibliographical references.
　ISBN 0-312-04793-2
　1. Providence and government of God. 2. Deism--Controversial literature. I. Title.
　BT96.2.S74 1990
　231.7--dc20　　　　　　　　　　　　　　　　　　　　　　90-43839
　　　　　　　　　　　　　　　　　　　　　　　　　　　　　CIP

Contents

List of Abbreviations	vi
Introduction	1

PART ONE
Consciousness	10
Rationality	29
Ethics	44
Will	54
Religion	68

Interlude: The Analogy of Human and Divine	80

PART TWO
Providence and Miracle	85
History	103
Prayer	116
Guidance	126
Grace	131
Revelation	141
Conclusion	152

PART ONE

List of Abbreviations

ET	English Translation
IVP	Inter-Varsity Press
SCM	Student Christian Movement
SPCK	Society for the Promotion of Christian Knowledge

Introduction

This essay is intended as a criticism of a particular view of God and the world, and the relationship between them, which has been explicitly avowed by several Christian theologians (differing considerably in their views on other matters) and is, I suspect, lurking in the back of the minds of a good many who are not theologians. I can best bring out what this view is by quoting from some of the theologians I have in mind. Here is, for instance, the late Rudolf Bultmann:

> The thought of the action of God as an unworldly and transcendent action can be protected from misunderstanding only if it is not thought of as an action which happens between the worldly actions and events, but as happening within them. The close connection between natural and historical events remains intact as it presents itself to the observer...This is the paradox of faith, that faith "nevertheless" understands as God's action here and now an event which is completely intelligible in the natural or historical connection of events.[1]

Here again is the Dutch Roman Catholic theologian, Piet Schoonenberg: 'God never works by intervention, in the stead of creatures...on the contrary, he realises all through making his world realise itself.'[2]

Professor Maurice Wiles, an Anglican, writes: 'Talk of God's activity is to be understood as a way of speaking about those events within the natural order or within human history in which God's purpose finds clear expression or special opportunity. Such a view...refrains from claiming any effective causation on the part of God in relation to particular occurrences.'[3] (By denying 'effective causation' Wiles does not of course mean that God tries but is *in*effective; he means that God does not 'effect' any one event more than another.)

An American, Dr Schubert M. Ogden, who has been associated with the 'process theology' school, can say that 'our picture of the world as a lawfully regulated whole and our understanding of our own self as a closed inner unity...imply both the empirical falsity of all mythology and its existential irrelevance, insofar as it is taken to to express a strictly empirical kind of truth.'[4] ('Mythology' here, as so often nowadays, is used in a sense which includes a large part of traditional Christian doctrine.)

And, finally, another Anglican, who is also a practising scientist, Dr A.C. Peacocke, can speak of 'the seamless character of the web which has been spun on the loom of time'[5] and describes 'interventionist assumptions about God's action in the world' as 'inconsistent and incoherent with what the sciences show about the way the world actually goes and with the way God actually seems to be creating new entities in the world'.[6]

These authors do not of course form a single homogeneous group; nor do I wish to suggest that they, or others who think in similar ways, hold too rigidly to the views expressed in these quotations. For instance, Dr Peacocke allows the possibility of 'specific revelatory acts of God towards men both in nature and history';[7] and Professor Wiles agrees that the emergence of the human race implies genuine novelty. Moreover, he believes strongly in human freedom to act on the world.[8] But in these quotations at least, in which they do seem to be expressing the general pattern of their thoughts, all for the moment endorse the view that the whole of what goes on in the universe (including that little bit of it which constitutes the human race) can be seen as an unbroken and continuous web of events governed by natural laws in which it is a mistake to look for special actions that can be ascribed to the God whom all believe to have created the web in the first place. I am going to call this sort of view 'continuism'. I might have used 'deism', recalling the eighteenth-century movement which took an almost identical view of the relationship between God and the world (as Wiles points out); but the deists' starting-point was a great confidence in the human intellect's power to understand God without the need of such superstitious ideas as revelation. I do not think the modern continuists are quite so sure of themselves. Moreover, many of them are clear that God is not only the creator but the sustainer of the universe, and not all the old deists realised this. In both respects, these theologians' position is an improvement on deism, and deserves a new name.

What, then, is their starting-point, if it is not confidence in the human intellect? What is the attraction of continuism, not only to radically-minded theologians, but (without necessarily being put into words) to a good many less intellectually gifted people, some in and many more outside the Churches? (For let us not forget that a vague, undogmatic belief in – not perhaps the God and Father of our Lord Jesus Christ, but certainly in *a* God – is very common among those who make no practice of Christianity or of any other religion; and the God of such people is often one who seldom or never intervenes in actual life.) I suspect that continuism gets its strength from three main sources – a belief about God, a belief about the world, and a belief about their proper relationship.

First, there is the experience of many who have been brought up as Christian believers, and whose spiritual life has been of the kind sometimes known as 'once-born'. There has been no divine onslaught on their lives, changing and disrupting everything, of the kind there was with Augustine, or Bernard, or Luther. The 'once-born' thinker, wrote N.P. Williams, would 'rule out of the category of possible modes of the Divine action all such as would come under the head of "undue influence" in a testamentary lawsuit; and, like Pelagius of old, would confine the meaning of grace to those Divine procedures which may be deemed to appeal to the rational understanding, such as the bestowal of information as to the contents of the moral law and the provision of object-lessons of virtue'.[9] Continuism takes this a step further. The supernatural bestowing of information or provision of examples is as uncomfortable an idea to them as that of overwhelming grace. If we cannot take 'undue influence' from the deity, we cannot take it even at second hand. If there has been no divine onslaught on my life, and yet God loves me, then there is no reason to think there has ever been any onslaught on anyone whom He loved. We not only can, we should get by without heavenly irruptions into our lives.

Second, and perhaps most important, there is a fully justified respect for the amazing achievements of modern science, which quite easily shifts into the not so justified notion that the necessary assumptions of scientific procedure must be the basic truth about the way the world has to be. As science habitually looks for laws and regularities (including of course statistical ones), it naturally assumes that they are there to be looked for; apparent singularities and one-off events are something of an embarrassment (witness the popularity, for completely non-scientific reasons, of 'oscillating universe' theories which avoid a unique 'big bang'), and the correct procedure, if they cannot be ignored, is to look for ways in which they may after all be subsumed under some general rule. This is perfectly proper procedure. But it does not entail that there are in actual fact no singularities or one-off events – including, it may be, some which are the work of God acting in a less regular manner than is His normal custom. It is easy, however, to assume that scientific procedure does entail precisely that, to turn a rule of method into a metaphysical principle. After all, if the metaphysical principle were true, it would clearly justify the rule of method; but the rule of method is clearly justified, as practice shows, so the metaphysical principle is true: the classical logical fallacy of 'affirming the consequent'. (If it were true that the sun went round the earth, we should see it rise and set; now we do see it rise and set; so...) Procedures, even quite proper procedures, do not yield universal truths. It is the proper procedure for a judge, faced with a disputed point of law, to look for precedents; but it does not follow that there will be precedents for every possible situation that may find its way into the courts. We must agree that enormous amounts of regularity have been found in the world; it is clear that the Creator does normally work by laws; it is not unnatural to suppose that He *always* does, that we have a 'lawfully regulated whole', a 'seamless web'. But however *natural*, it is not *necessary*.

A third reason which may have influenced some continuists is this. Those who are *not* continuists are apt to write in terms of 'interventions' by God in the world. I shall be doing so myself in what follows. Now the picture this suggests is of God and the world as two distinct entities, almost unrelated to one another, but with one of them (God) interfering from time to time with the other; rather like (it has been suggested to me) a school-teacher intervening when a fight breaks out among the children during break. Now this is not in the least the true picture of the relationship between God and His creation. God is constantly sustaining the world by His loving and creative power; He is not distanced from it. If this is a source of continuism, it is a source which has every right to be there. God is *not* distanced from us, nor from the rest of His works. He is a God near at hand. But this truth is not, surely, one to be protected by distancing Him *further* from His creation, in practice if not in theory, so that *all* He does is sustain it! Nevertheless, the criticism implied of much non-continuist language is quite justified. If I use words like 'intervene' in what follows, it is not because I regard God as behaving like our school-teacher; it is for lack of a better word to refer to those actions of God which do not fall into the regular pattern in which He sustains the world. He is at all times close to us; in Him we live and move and have our being; but (I believe) that does not mean that He cannot be actively concerned with the changes of His world, responding, even in 'irregular' ways, to what goes on in it.

In his Bampton Lectures, Professor Wiles advanced another, more philosophical reason for continuism. It is an interesting one, and worth looking at, though it has not as far as I know influenced anyone apart from Professor Wiles himself, and should not perhaps be reckoned as a 'source' of continuism like the others we have been considering. An *act*, Wiles points out, involves an intention and a goal. 'To call something "an act", then, is to give a unity to what would otherwise appear only as random occurrences, and to do so by bringing them together as contributing to some overall intention. [Therefore] the primary usage for the idea of divine action should be in relation to the world as a whole rather than to particular occurrences within it.'[10] This does not mean that just because we believe God to be the Creator of the whole we must of necessity rule out the idea of divine action in particular occurrences – this is discussed in the rest of Wiles' book; but it gives us a presumption, it suggests that we should not naturally *expect* particular actions on God's part.

The trouble is that the conclusion does not really follow from the premiss. If God were limited to one act or one intention, it would be correct. But Wiles himself very rightly observes that the creation and fulfilment of men and women can hardly be claimed to be the only divine intention; at least, not without being unduly anthropocentric. 'There may be other intentions of which we are in no position to know anything.'[11] The scale of creation in time and space suggests to me that there probably *are*. And even in human terms there are, one would imagine, as many intentions as there are people, since God intends fulfilment for everyone (whether or not that intention can be carried out in the face of human rejection). So that while creation is no doubt to be conceived of as a single act (although an eternal or timeless one), that act may have been in the nature of an essential condition for the achieving of a large number of divine intentions, each of which might – though of course this may not always be the case – require other acts to bring it about.

Wiles' illustration of an 'act' – the potting of a billiard ball – rather makes my point. The player has in fact a number of related intentions. There is the ultimate intention of winning the game; there are subordinate intentions of scoring well in each of a series of breaks; and there are individual intentions of making this particular ball here and now drop into this particular pocket. We may for many purposes treat 'playing a game of billiards' as a single act; but for other purposes we may wish to treat it as a varying number of separate acts. And so, far from the fact that the game, treated as a unity, eliminates the possibility of single small-scale acts, the game actually *requires* such acts. This is of course because billiards is played the way it is. It may be that the divine act of creation is such that it does not require, or even permit, any subordinate actions. But this needs to be shown! The unity of creation does not in itself say anything at all, one way or the other, about divine actions within that unity. There is no presumption in favour of continuism to be derived from the nature of an 'act'.

Perhaps we ought to add one last possible cause of continuism to our list. That is quite simply the breakdown of the traditional Christian view of the world and God's dealings with it. Two hundred years ago, Christians (though not of course the deists of those days, nor indeed many others affected by the Enlightenment) took it for granted that the Bible was to be accepted as literal truth throughout, and the work of such traditional authors as Moses and David; that the world was about six thousand years old; that miracles had been common, at least in Biblical times and perhaps since then as well (Protestant and Catholic might have differed there); that other religions were at best superstition and at worst deliberate deceptions, the work of Satan; and so on. The increase of knowledge, not only in the sciences but also in such areas as Biblical criticism and comparative religion, has made it very difficult to hold such a view today. Now part of this discarded view was the belief that God habitually acted in the world in discontinuous ways – not only in spectacular miracle but in grace, in unobtrusive providences, in revelation, and so on. And if the old view as a whole needed to be replaced, why not this part of it?

Basically, because in the other areas the change was brought about by genuine advances in knowledge. It really did become very hard (except for a few really determined conservatives) to believe that the earth was only six thousand years old, because of the work of geologists; it really did become very hard to believe that Moses wrote the Pentateuch, or Matthew the first Gospel, in the light of Biblical scholarship; it really did become very hard to dismiss, say, Buddhism as idolatrous or even diabolical in the light of greater knowledge of its founder and its thought. But the rejection of divine activity in the world did not rest on any new discovery of this sort. (Though the converse is perhaps to some extent true; some of the theories that were devised during this period, especially the more radical ones, may well have been inspired, consciously or unconsciously, by 'continuist' ideas in the back of their devisers' minds.) Continuism is a further, and not necessarily a warranted, step.

In sum I believe continuism, whatever the sources of its appeal, to be quite mistaken. In the present essay I wish to argue, first, that human life itself cannot be made sense of on a continuist basis. For the most part I shall be considering human life from the standpoint of a Christian, for the continuists I have been quoting are all avowed Christians; to try to argue against atheist or agnostic continuists at the same time would involve one in a full-scale apologetics, for obviously defences are open to an atheist which are not open to Christians, however radical. If my arguments do tell against non-Christian continuism, so much the better; but that is not their immediate purpose.

I hope, secondly, to go on to consider what kinds of 'discontinuities' are needed by Christianity in its attempts to understand a little of the divine life and activity, as well as the human. There is a faint parallel here to something that happened in the original deist controversy. The most famous criticism of the deists was that of Butler in his *Analogy of Religion to the Constitution and Course of Nature*, in which he argued that 'if there be an analogy or likeness between that system of things and dispensation of Providence, which revelation informs us of, and that system of things and dispensation of Providence, which experience together with reason informs us of, *i.e.* the known course of Nature; this is a presumption, that they have both the same author and cause'. I do not for a moment claim the profundity or historical importance of Butler's great work, but

I do hope to show that the system of things which experience and reason inform us of in human life is analogous in many ways to the system of things which Christian faith, based on the Scriptures, believes to be true of part of the divine life.

Notes

1. *Jesus Christ and Mythology* (ET London, SCM, 1960), pp. 61, 65

2. *The Christ* (ET London, Sheed & Ward, 1972), p. 21

3. *The Remaking of Christian Doctrine* (London, SCM, 1974), p. 38

4. *The Point of Christology* (London, SCM, 1982), p. 6

5. *Creation and the World of Science* (Oxford, Clarendon, 1979), p. 60

6. Op. cit., p. 134

7. Op. cit., p. 357

8. Personal communication, 13 August, 1982. Cf. also *God's Action in the World* (London, SCM, 1986), p. 65: 'The world we know is not a closed, deterministically ordered system.'

9. *The Grace of God* (pbk edn, London, Hodder & Stoughton, 1966), p. 11

10. *God's Action in the World* (London, SCM, 1986), p. 28

11. Ibid., p. 30

PART ONE

Consciousness

Our first evidence for discontinuity in the world will be the existence of *consciousness* or *awareness*. I shall try and explain as clearly as I can what I mean by this. I do not mean the property of being conscious as opposed to asleep, stunned, or under the influence of an anaesthetic; nor the property of being aware or conscious of one particular object. 'Consciousness' in the sense in which I should like to use the word can be present even during sleep, provided that one is dreaming, and it need not be of any object in the sense of a material body. Perhaps what I mean can best be grasped by imagining a robot that was constructed to behave just like a human being. It would react to sounds and sights and smells in just the same way as you or I would (with one important reservation which we shall come to later). But there would be no mental events going on in the robot's 'life': nothing but the external events and its reactions to them, including of course its verbal reactions when it spoke or wrote. It is the mental events that the robot would not have, but that we certainly do have, which constitute a large part of what I mean by 'consciousness'. We not only react to our surroundings; we are *aware* of them.

Philosophers have developed a special vocabulary – indeed, more than one, at different times – to enable them to talk about the phenomena of consciousness. Thus David Hume, at the beginning of his *Treatise of Human Nature*, states that 'all the perceptions of the human mind resolve themselves into two distinct kinds, which I shall call *impressions* and *ideas*', defining 'impressions' as 'all our sensations, passions and emotions, as they make their first appearance in the soul', and 'ideas' as 'the faint images of these in thinking and reasoning'. These latter would include the mental images we can conjure up when asked to close our eyes and (say) imagine a white cup and a blue saucer, or which come to us unbidden in dreams. These clearly are no part of an external object in space (a real cup, for example); yet they have relationships which are not unlike those which real objects seem to have. The imagined cup may, for instance, be imagined as on the saucer much as a real cup may be seen to be on a real saucer. In imagining or dreaming we are conscious (in my sense of the word), yet not conscious of anything in the world around us. Hume's 'impressions' are also part of 'consciousness' in my sense; they are not a part of the world about us any more than a mental image is, but they can have the same sort of relationships as mental images can. My 'impression' or 'perception' of a cup may be 'above' that of a saucer – even if in fact I am seeing them in a concave mirror and in reality it is the saucer which is above the cup.

I can see one difficulty here. We may be tempted to say that our humanoid robot could also have 'impressions'. Would it not report that the image of the cup in the mirror was above that of the saucer? If it had been given a head shaped like ours, would it not report the existence of two 'ghostly noses' like the ones that we live with all our days, one seen by each eye? And if so, does this not undermine what I have been saying? for surely there would be no strange discontinuity about our robot.

I think that it would *not* undermine it: or, rather, that the imaginary picture it paints of life with robots is inaccurate. This is where the reservation I spoke of earlier comes in. I doubt if the robot *would* speak in the way we do about our experiences, the way we have just been imagining it to speak. It would report that the part of the mirror reflecting the cup was above the part reflecting the saucer; it would report that it could see the left-hand side of its nose with its left eye and the right-hand side with its right, and that this did not prevent it from seeing objects hidden from one eye by its nose. But that it would begin to talk in terms of 'images' and 'ghostly noses', let alone develop a vocabulary of 'ideas' and 'impressions' or the equivalent – this seems to me most unlikely, unless indeed it had been specially programmed to do so (in which case it would no longer be the truthful robot it once was), or had by some miracle acquired a 'consciousness', and become no longer a robot but a person.

This is where it seems to me that Professor Hilary Putnam has erred. In his *Mind, Language and Reality*[1] he pointed out correctly that a robot might learn to report that something had looked red although in actual fact it wasn't. It might, he went on, argue 'When I have the illusion that something red is present, nothing red is physically there. Yet, in a sense, I *see* something red. What I see, I *call* a sense-datum.' But this needs arguing for, and Putnam simply takes it for granted as one of a list of possible philosophical developments among sophisticated robots. The robot would *not*, surely, say that 'in a sense' it saw something red; all it would say is that the (real, physical) thing *looked* red or *seemed* red.

However, that the phenomena I have been trying to indicate do exist among human beings can hardly be denied, even if exactly how to describe and analyse them is and has been for many years a matter of dispute. And that they are there is what I mean to assert in claiming that there is such a thing as 'consciousness'. I say 'can hardly be denied'. The only group which might possibly deny it is that of the 'behaviourists', and many even of them would probably only deny the *importance* of consciousness. Behaviourism originated as a proposal for psychological method: since introspection of one's feelings and sensations seemed not to get psychology very far, why not *ignore* feelings and sensations and concentrate on the study, prediction and control of behaviour? And certainly if a behaviourist claims that by doing this he or she can (for instance) train pigeons to aim bombs, there is no reason to doubt this. If, however, behaviourists proceed to the further claim, as some apparently have, that mental events do not exist at all (the self, according to one distinguished member of the school, is 'a device for representing a functionally unified system of responses'[2]), they are obviously talking nonsense. That benefactor of humanity who first discovered that quinine could be used to treat malaria knew nothing of the existence of the malarial parasite, but could ignore such matters and concentrate on the prediction and control of the illness. But he or she would have been wrong to deny that any parasite in the bloodstream existed!

Indeed, one of the strongest arguments against behaviourism is, paradoxically enough, that it is actually true sometimes – and only sometimes. A lot of our actions really are automatic, including quite complex ones. Many motorists must have had the alarming experience of suddenly realising that they have been driving for several miles without being aware of it, because their thoughts were elsewhere. They had adjusted speed and steering quite correctly without being conscious (in my sense) of the conditions they were adjusting them to, or of the fact that they *were* adjusting them. They had been Behaviourist People with no (relevant) 'inner life'. But of course this is not universal; and if behaviourism were true it would have to be. There is of course the interesting possibility that behaviourists themselves do *not* have any 'consciousness', and therefore jump to the conclusion that nobody else has any either; like the people in H.G. Wells' *The Country of the Blind* who, when an outsider came across their community, could not believe at first that such a thing as sight existed. It has been known for a long time that there are people who have little or no power of forming mental images; perhaps there are some who simply do react to the external world without being 'conscious', who are in effect protoplasmic robots. If so, one may offer them sympathy for their unknowingly impoverished lives; but one must not allow them to bully the rest of us into pretending a similar poverty.

Behaviourism is not the only kind of materialist 'philosophy of mind' that there is. Others have been devised; and a very popular one in recent years has been the 'mind/brain identity theory', which holds that mental events like perceptions, while real enough, are actually *identical* with physical events going on in the brains of those doing the perceiving. Whether or not the theory overall is valid, the point to be made here is that it does not deny the existence of consciousness; what it does deny is the existence of a special sort of *thing*, the mind or soul, to be that which *has* consciousness. It prefers to ascribe consciousness directly to the brain. Brain events (according to this theory) have their normal physical characteristics and relationships, but some of them also have 'mental' ones, and it is this fact which is represented by the statement that 'there is such a thing as "consciousness" '.

But in consciousness we have something which is not itself physical. Either it is a property of a non-physical thing, the mind or soul, or it is a shorthand way of referring to a variety of non-physical qualities of certain events in the brain. Either way, it seems to form a breach in the continuity of events. For on the latter hypothesis certain physical events have acquired properties which are of a quite different type from those we can detect in the rest of the world, and on the former a non-physical entity has come into existence in, or at least closely bound up with, the physical universe.

Nor can we say that while 'mental events' exist, they do not affect the physical world, and therefore do not disturb its continuity. For while in theory it might be possible to maintain that most of our conscious planning, thinking, deliberating, and so on is a mere by-product of the functioning of the brain, and in no way affects it (and there are serious problems with this apart from its initial implausibility, as we shall see in later chapters), there is one way in which consciousness quite certainly affects the physical world, and that is in cases where (as in this present chapter) we actually discuss consciousness itself. For if it did not affect the world *at all*, we should have to suppose that all these discussions of consciousness would have happened even if no such thing had existed. We should all be solemnly discussing it as if it were something real whether it was or it wasn't. Indeed, even if it did exist, there would be no way to tell that it did except in oneself; for the assertion by anyone else that they were conscious would not have been caused by their actually *being* conscious, and would thus be wholly unreliable. In this particular area, and therefore quite possibly in others, consciousness affects the continuity of the physical world.

Can these arguments be countered? I can see one way in which it might theoretically be done. We said above that brain events must have acquired non-physical properties or a non-physical entity have come into existence. But suppose the expressions 'acquired' and 'have come' were mistaken? All that has been proved is that certain physical events *have* properties which are not physical, or that a non-physical entity *now* exists. It could be that these properties or entities have *always* existed, instead of coming into existence only with the arrival of the human brain. Something along these lines was evidently held by Teilhard de Chardin: 'Every element of the Universe contains, at least to an infinitesimal degree, some germ of inwardness and spontaneity, that is to say of consciousness.'[3] If this is the case, it would not be surprising if certain factors (physical factors, like the size and complexity of the brain) enabled those infinitesimal germs of consciousness to coalesce into something far from infinitesimal, like the conscious life of an adult human being. And in that case consciousness would always have been a fully functioning part of the universe; continuity would not have quite the shape we thought it had, but it would be there. The point about the effect consciousness has on the physical world would remain valid, but perhaps physical and non-physical could be seen as parts of a single whole which (viewed *as* a whole) would be continuous. And certainly the point about the origin of consciousness would have been met.

Now I do not really think that this proposed 'continuity within the whole' would satisfy actual continuists. Their position, as I said earlier, draws much of its strength from the picture of the world suggested by the physical sciences; and this is not the picture of a whole in which physical events, or certain classes of them, are constantly affected by mental ones. (I am not, of course, trying to argue that the physical sciences are misleading or misguided, only that they do not give a complete picture.) But in any case there is an obvious difficulty with the Teilhardian picture. How does one detect these infinitesimal germs of consciousness? It is hard enough to prove that other human beings are conscious in our special sense of the word; as we have noted, it may be that there are some who are *not*. How far down the scale of animal life is consciousness normally supposed to exist? Some animals, such as dogs, appear to dream, which suggests consciousness in our sense; but so far as I know there is no actual evidence that this is so with tapeworms or jellyfish. Still less is there any to suggest even an infinitesimal germ of consciousness in a pebble or a beer-bottle.

Now this does not mean that no such germ exists. It only means that there is no empirical evidence to show that it does. But a further difficulty does seem to afford positive reason to doubt the reality of these 'germs'; and that is the problem of imagining just what a 'germ of consciousness' could *be*. With matter there is no difficulty in conceiving of smaller and smaller quantities. A mouse clearly contains less matter than a mountain, and more than a microbe. That the process cannot continue indefinitely is not a logical truth, it is a scientific discovery. But can we do anything like this with consciousness? We can of course suppose a being with fewer senses than we have; indeed, we do not need to 'suppose' them, for they exist. The blind and the deaf are in this sense (though hardly in any other) 'less conscious' than the rest of us. But clearly this will not get us very far towards the 'infinitesimal germ'.

Or again, we may suppose a being with much more *restricted* senses and consciousness than we have, like someone with 'tunnel vision' or a limited range of hearing; or for that matter with a human sense of smell contrasted with that of a dog. This could be imagined on a much more serious scale, so that only a very small visual field or range of sounds would be perceived. (Of course, actual tunnel vision and limited hearing are the results of defects in the physical system of the eyes and ears, and non-living matter *has* no eyes or ears, if we ignore corpses; indeed, many living creatures do not have them. But then some of these are sensitive to light and sound, so this is no fatal difficulty.) Again, some creatures' senses are less efficient at discrimination than others'; and this too could be on a very serious scale. It might be that this, or something like it, is actually the case with some forms of life – those, for instance, which are sensitive to light although lacking eyes. There are problems here, though. This is just the kind of area where a 'behaviourist' account begins to look more attractive. If a flower opens to the sun, and this can be explained in terms of its physiology and chemistry alone, there seems to be no reason to suppose that there is consciousness present (though doubtless there *might* be). Moreover, in creatures where consciousness does exist, such as human beings, there are many reactions to stimuli like light which do not involve it, like the contraction of the pupil of the eye when light becomes brighter; and it seems quite likely that the reactions of plants and lower animals are of this kind. We cannot therefore say with any confidence that sensitivity to light implies, or even suggests, a restricted consciousness. It may be possible, but such analogies as can be drawn with our own functioning suggest that it is not in fact true.

And all this is where we are dealing with things that are unquestionably alive. What possible meaning can there be in ascribing consciousness to pebbles – even consciousness of a most rudimentary kind? It makes sense to imagine that such things are *fully* aware (though not much sense to believe it). But what could a 'rudimentary' awareness be like? Something like what we have on the borderland between waking and sleeping, or what we may suppose a new-born baby has? But surely even these are too much to ascribe to our pebble. And yet how can there be a consciousness that is less than these which can still be called a consciousness, or even the infinitesimal germ of one?

The only answer that occurs to me is that which was put forward (for different reasons) by Leibniz.[4] In his view, there are 'monads' or simple substances everywhere, which 'perceive', that is, represent, the world outside them. Perhaps the simplest way to convey what Leibniz was getting at would be something like this. If you and I are looking at the same scene six feet apart from one another, we shall see it slightly differently. The differences will be greatest with things close to us; you will see your hands quite differently from the way I see them, but our versions of the clouds in the sky above us will be just about indistinguishable. Now half-way between us there is a rosebush.

There is an 'aspect' of the scene from where that rosebush is, just as there is from where you and I are. And Leibniz is in effect saying that this 'aspect' is 'perceived' by the monads which make up the rosebush. (Each of these differs of course from the others, but that need not concern us now.) The rosebush differs from you and me in that it cannot remember its perceptions, nor can it (in Leibniz' phrase) 'apperceive', that is, be aware of its own inner states. Here, perhaps, we have our 'infinitesimal germ' of consciousness. Yet it is interesting that Leibniz reserved the word 'conscious' for those monads which could apperceive; and when he notes that conscious beings can come into the condition of 'simple monads' at times, what he has in mind is states like a deep dreamless sleep. And if that is all that can be ascribed to the inanimate world, I doubt if continuity can be saved after all. There seems to be a difference in kind as well as in degree between the state of a simple monad (or a normally conscious being in a deep dreamless sleep) and a conscious being awake, or dreaming. And we might note that when Bertrand Russell in 1914 sought to develop a more up-to-date version of the Leibnizian position,[5] he did so in terms of 'sensibilia' which did not need to be attached to any mind, and added the significant comment 'What the mind adds to *sensibilia*, in fact, is *merely* awareness.' So even here, it seems, where there has been a sustained effort to fill the world with aspects or viewpoints, the notion of awareness or consciousness forces its way in and spoils the continuity.

It seems to me, then, quite certain that at some point or points in the past our ancestors became 'aware' or 'conscious' in the sense I have been using the words, even though at previous times they or their predecessors had been no such thing. The process may have been gradual; the border between sleeping and wakefulness is not always a sharp one, and that between unawareness and the full awareness we possess may not have been sharp either. But at the end of the process there was something new in the world, a conscious human being, and at the beginning there had not been.

A Christian may be inclined to associate with this process

such passages as Genesis 1:27 and 2:7, in which man is said to have been created in the image and likeness of God, or to have become a living soul. But for our present purposes it is not necessary to do so. We are not at the moment concerned with the action of God in the world, but with the life of human beings. I do myself think it likely that 'consciousness' was indeed the special creation of the Lord; but if we set this aside as undecidable, does it make any difference? (To the question of discontinuity in the world, that is; obviously it makes a difference to our theology.)

Suppose, for instance, that it is claimed that evolution will explain the existence of consciousness. Will that enable us to avoid the discontinuity? William James, I understand,[6] suggested that consciousness would be of considerable evolutionary value, enabling the steering of a nervous system too complicated to regulate itself. Similarly, we find Sir Karl Popper suggesting that 'consciousness grows from small beginnings; perhaps its first form is a vague feeling of irritation, experienced when the organism has a problem to solve such as getting away from an irritant substance... Consciousness will assume evolutionary significance – and increasing significance – when it begins to *anticipate* possible ways of reacting.'[7] But it does not seem that a 'behaviourist' organism would be any worse off than a conscious one; its life would be different, but not surely in any way that would be relevant to natural selection. For example, it would lack the mental events that we call experiences of pleasure and pain; but it would seek pleasure and avoid pain in just the same way that we do. It might even have a slight advantage in so far as it was not distracted by introspection. Professor Thorpe remarks that James' suggestion 'now sounds to us very naïve; so much of the complex steering systems of the higher animals having been explained on reasonably self-regulating and automatic bases'.[8] But even if James were right it would not affect the basic point. Natural selection would in such a case lead to the preservation and possibly the prevalence of consciousness; it could not bring it into being. Where did the 'vague feeling of irritation' come from? Or, rather, *how* did it come? Even if this is ascribed to some kind of mutation, that makes no difference to the present stage of the argument. For whereas other mutations produce changes in anatomy or physiology – in size, let us say, or in resistance to disease – this one must be supposed to have introduced an entirely new element into the life of the organism, one wholly indescribable in physical terms. The novelty, the discontinuity is there, whether the change was brought about by a mutation or by divine fiat (or of course by some other method). I must admit that I myself find the idea of a mutation with this sort of effect impossible to believe in, but even if I am utterly mistaken in this, it makes no actual difference; the discontinuity is just as great. 'Mutation', after all, means 'change', and the change we have here in the appearance of consciousness is one that is discontinuous with everything that preceded it.

It might be thought that appeal to the existence of *holistic* qualities (that is, qualities belonging to a whole but not to any of its parts) might save continuism. For no continuist will deny that holistic qualities come into existence and pass out of it again quite abruptly, or think of this fact as undermining the continuist position. *Waking* and *sleeping* are both holistic qualities of living animals. (So indeed is the quality of *being a living animal* itself, which is lost when the animal dies.) If continuism can accommodate these, why not consciousness?

Mainly because while living, waking, sleeping and other qualities are not definable in terms of the parts of the whole to which they apply, nevertheless they are physical terms, describing patterns of movement and the like. Although a particular pattern of movement may come into existence and pass out of it again very abruptly, movement itself (including the movement of the physical objects involved in the pattern) does not do so. But consciousness, in the sense in which we have been using the term, though it may be an holistic quality, is different in kind from these other holistic qualities. If I nod asleep over a book, my 'awakeness' ends; I no longer turn the pages or follow the lines of print with my eyes, but I continue to breathe, toss in my sleep, and so on. Even if I die, my body may slump to the floor or be borne off by sorrowing relatives. One pattern of physical events has been replaced by another. But if I cease to be conscious, there is no pattern of anything that succeeds this; and if I become conscious, there is no pattern of anything that preceded it.

We may look briefly at three further attempts to save universal continuity – or rather, at three views of the nature of mind which might be used in such an attempt. Firstly, since the rise of computers into the general consciousness, some have wanted to suggest that while the brain corresponds to the 'hardware' of a computer, the mind corresponds, not to some kind of non-physical hardware, but to the 'software', the programs in accordance with which the computer functions.[9] 'We never ask "How does a computer program make its circuits solve the equation?" Nor do we need to ask how thoughts trigger neurons to produce bodily responses.'[10]

The distinction between hardware and software is of course an interesting and important one; but I cannot see that it is in any way relevant to the nature of mind. A brain might quite easily operate according to rules that did not mention neurons, nodes and the like, but were expressed wholly in 'higher-level' language; but where would the idea of consciousness come in? The programs according to which the brain operates (if that is a proper way to describe it) are formal procedures: they are not awarenesses, thoughts, acts of will or anything like that. Conversely, awarenesses, thoughts, and similar 'mental events' are, precisely, events; they are located in time just as much as the triggering of neurons. But programs and software are not events, nor do they consist of such. Indeed, if the mind really were a separate entity altogether from the brain, it would surely have itself its own 'software' of procedures whereby it operated; and if it did, it would be distinct from this software!

A more general argument related to this last is that 'mind' and 'body' are in some sense *complementary* aspects of a single unity. The late Professor D.M. Mackay was an eloquent propounder of this argument, and he wrote as a Christian, and an orthodox Christian at that, as well as as a scientist. We need not look to computers for examples of the sort of complementary descriptions he had in mind. A ship's lamp-signals convey a message to the trained eye; to the untrained they are just a series of flashes of light. The two descriptions in no way contradict one another. Yet if the viewer reads them as a message, 'it is not as if he had found something mysterious going on *as well as* the flashing...The message is related to the flashing of light, not as an effect is to a cause, but rather as one aspect of a complex unity is related to another aspect.'[11]

Once again, we have a truth but not a relevant truth. It is perfectly true that ships' signals, and many other things, can be studied from the point of view of a physicist and of a message-receiver, and that these do not interfere with one another. But what needs to be proved is that this explains or accounts for the thing I have been calling 'consciousness', and it doesn't. For one thing alone, the complementarity arises even with the 'behaviourist's dream', a person who has no inner life. For our outward behaviour considered by itself is both a series of physical events and also something which should be described in terms of a 'complex unity'. If I hurry downstairs and answer the telephone, I behave as a physical system, and also as a person; the two descriptions do not conflict in the least: but we have said nothing about my being 'conscious' in the sense that word is being used here. (It is significant that Sir Peter Strawson, whose book *Individuals*[12] took a line in many ways similar to the one we are discussing, distinguished, not between material and mental predicates, but between material and *personal* ones; and he seems to me to be much closer to the mark than MacKay and his followers.) But the moment we start to describe my inner sensations, imaginings and so forth, we find we are describing something which cannot be treated as 'personal' in the outward and visible sense that hurrying downstairs can. We need a *third* level of description. Unless indeed we take it that 'mental' descriptions are complementary to physical ones, not of the whole human being as a complex unity, but of the brain; and in that case we are back with the 'mind/brain identity theory' referred to earlier.

Nor will it do to invoke the idea of 'emergence'. C.D. Broad distinguished[13] between four possible views of the nature of mind. First, that it is an illusion. Secondly, that, though real, it can be 'reduced' to matter (or some other sort of entity), that is, can be understood purely in terms of it, rather in the way in which the movement of a queue can be understood in terms of the movements of the individual people in it. Thirdly, that it is a thing in its own right, a 'substance'. And fourthly, that it is 'emergent'. An 'emergent' characteristic is, roughly speaking, a property held by a class of things, which cannot be understood, and whose presence in those things could not be predicted, purely on a basis of knowledge of the component parts of the things (taken separately, that is, or in other combinations). Broad's tentative example is the way in which salt has properties, such as its taste, which could not be predicted from our knowledge of sodium alone, or chlorine alone, or of other compounds of those elements. In our present case, the suggestion might be that mind 'emerges' whenever the brain reaches a certain level of development. We do not need to suppose divine intervention to produce it, any more than we need to suppose divine intervention to produce the taste of salt; it is a law of nature that whenever you have a brain of such-and-such a level of development, you have the events that we group together for convenience's sake and call a 'mind' – many of which are of course 'conscious' experiences. A Christian or other theist taking this line would of course ascribe this law to God, but it would not require a special act of creation for the first or any other 'conscious' mind.

There is no need to discuss the theory of 'emergence' here.[14] Suffice it to say that even if true it does not affect the main point I have been seeking to make. The theory does not deny discontinuity; indeed, it is positively *asserted*: all that the theory adds is that this discontinuity is always to be found in certain circumstances, that if (for example) beings with similarly developed brains exist on a small planet somewhere in the vicinity of Betelgeuse, they too will turn out to be 'conscious'. Physical nature is still acted upon by minds. We still live in a world that is a little jerky at times, not a smooth machine, even if the jerks follow a kind of pattern: God has made a discontinuous universe, even if it is one where some of the discontinuities are governed by law.

CONSCIOUSNESS AFTER DEATH

Christianity, like most of the world's religions, has taught that death is not the end of life, only of *this* life. Consciousness, in some form, continues or begins again; we exist without our mortal bodies or are raised to life with new, immortal ones. Most Christian continuists do not wish to deny this. Even Bultmann, who regarded all attempts to give *content* to the Christian's future as 'wishful images of imagination',[15] is firm that 'even in death, man is not released from the hand of God, and he has to encounter death as the encounter with God, for his salvation or his damnation'.[16] Now it might be thought that here we have a very serious element of discontinuity. What could break the closed web of this world more startlingly than the continuation of one of its elements – a human consciousness – into an existence quite outside the web, except perhaps the miraculous resurrection of such a consciousness in a new body within it?

I imagine that a continuist might reply somewhat along these lines: The General Resurrection (if indeed it is not to be regarded simply as a vivid mythical presentation of an undefined hope for the future) is *not* within this world; even the Bible speaks of it in terms of 'a new heaven and a new earth'.[17] The General Resurrection does not, then, affect the continuity of the present world. But no more does the idea of an enduring consciousness after death. The closed web is no more disrupted by the death of a human being than by that of a plant, even if it be true that something (a 'future life') begins *outside* the web when a human dies, and not when a plant does.

Such a reply has some validity, but I am not sure how much. Either the human consciousness before death is part of the web or it is not. If it is not, then (according to the argument developed in the preceding chapter) it affects the web during its life, and at its death ceases to do so. And this does mean a discontinuity of a kind – a discontinuity by *subtraction* from the general pattern of things, not by addition to it. If, on the other hand, it is to be regarded as part of the web, then its continuance outside the web is clearly also a discontinuity by subtraction, and a greater one than in the first case: there seems to be no way out of the dilemma except denying the existence of consciousness after death – a perfectly valid move for the atheist, but hardly for the would-be Christian. I must admit, however, that as far as the General Resurrection is concerned the continuist has a point. Resurrection into another world might possibly be compatible with the 'scientific' motive for continuism; it would (if we are considering it entirely on its own) leave the general pattern of things undisturbed. But I doubt if it would fit in very well with the 'religious' motive.[18] If God loves me in such a way as to resurrect me in miraculous fashion, it is a little odd that this same love should firmly refrain from touching my life in less spectacular (though equally miraculous) fashion.

Perhaps this would be the place to raise one further point; although it might belong better in the second part of this book, which treats of divine activity, it is so closely linked with the question of consciousness after death that it is mentioned here instead. If there is any form of life after death, there was some first person who survived his or her death, before whom no-one did so. (Those who believe in a future life for animals other than human beings may substitute 'creature' for 'person' – it does not affect the argument.) God is not in that case related to the whole animal creation in a uniform way; He introduced novelty into it when He decided to bestow a new gift on this person (or creature), even though it was not a gift that could be detected in this world. Perhaps the continuist may feel that this last concession is all that is needed. The gift may be bestowed without disturbing anything in this universe. True. Yet it does mean that the Lord does not always act uniformly; there is nothing in His nature that obliges Him to maintain absolute continuity. And if this is so, may He not also break the continuity in other, more intramundane ways?

A SPECULATION

It is difficult to resist adding here a note on a subject which I have no real right to add notes on, but which is so fascinating to an outsider like myself that I made no great effort to resist. It arises from a well-known problem in the interpretation of quantum physics. In many cases, given a particular system, theory does not predict a straightforward and unambiguous outcome. Instead, it predicts a number of possible outcomes, each of which can be assigned a probability value only. Which possible outcome will actually occur can only be found by actual measurement. The question is, what do we say about the state immediately before the measurement? Do we say that if our measurement gave us a value X, X was the value beforehand, but it was inaccessible? Apparently there are considerable scientific difficulties with this view. Or do we say that the value was actually indeterminate until it was measured? Probably this was for a long time the most widely held view; perhaps it still is. But it gave rise to the notorious paradox of 'Schrödinger's cat'. Suppose that instead of taking a measurement we construct a system which has an even chance of starting or not starting a process which kills a cat, and observe the state of the cat. Can we really say that the state of the cat – whether it was alive or dead – was indeterminate until we observed it?

One solution to this is to say that where a number of possible outcomes are predicted, *all* are in fact fulfilled. (This is usually called the 'many-worlds interpretation', because it can be described as the formation of different worlds which diverge from one another – in this case, one where the cat is alive and one where it is not.) But another was made in a paper[19] by the distinguished physicist Eugene P. Wigner. In his imaginary experiment we have a device with a certain chance of giving off a flash at a moment t. A friend of ours is observing it, and we ask him what he has observed. Suppose he says he did see a flash.

That is fine; it is as if we had used some recording device and it had recorded a flash at time t. But suppose we now ask our friend, 'What did you feel about the flash before I asked you?' Surely he will answer 'I told you already, I did see a flash'? Nothing corresponds to this in the case of the recording device. Indeed, the mathematical formula which describes the probable states of the object which gives the flash plus those of the recording device is not the same as that describing the object *plus* our friend (unless we suppose that the friend was in a state of suspended animation before he answered!). 'It follows,' Wigner wrote, 'that the being with a consciousness must have a different role in quantum mechanics than the inanimate measuring device.'[20] Consciousness is affecting the physical world.

Wigner himself was perplexed by the problem of finding other ways to verify the thesis that consciousness affects the body as well as vice versa; and this has been heartily agreed with by critics of his position. 'There has been little progress beyond the speculation stage', comment Clifton and Regehr.[21] This is doubtless true. But perhaps the present essay may help. If so, Wigner's position and mine might lend one another mutual support.

Notes

1. Cambridge University Press, 1975; the reference is to pp. 387 ff.

2. Skinner, B.F., *Science and Human Behaviour* (New York, Macmillan, 1966), p. 285

3. *The Appearance of Man* (London, Collins, 1965), p. 139

4. *Principles of Nature and Grace*, secs 1-4; *Monadology*, secs 13-14

5. *Mysticism and Logic* (pbk edn, Harmondsworth, Penguin, 1953), pp. 142 ff.

6. Cited by Thorpe, W.H., *Animal Nature and Human Nature* (London, Methuen, 1974), p. 320

7. *Objective Knowledge* (rev. edn, Oxford University Press, 1979), pp. 250-1

8. Thorpe, loc. cit.

9. E.g. Davies, P., *God and the New Physics* (pbk edn, Harmonds-worth, 1983), pp. 85 ff.

10. Davies, op. cit., p. 86

11. *Christianity in a Mechanistic Universe* (London, IVP, 1965), pp. 57-8

12. London, Methuen, 1959; ch. 3, esp. pp. 103 ff.

13. *The Mind and its Place in Nature* (London, Routledge, 1925), pp. 607 ff.

14. For discussion of it I would refer the reader to Broad, op. cit., chapter 2, and to Pap, A., *Introduction to the Philosophy of Science* (London, Eyre and Spottiswoode, 1963) pp. 364 ff.

15. *Expository Times*, vol. 65, 1954, p. 278

16. *Kerygma and Myth*, I (ET London, SPCK, 1953), p. 205

17. Isaiah 65:17 and 66:22; 2 Peter 2:13; Revelation 21:1

18. See p. 3 above

19. In *The scientist speculates*, ed. Good (London, Heinemann, 1962), pp. 284 ff.

20. Wigner, op. cit., p. 294

21. 'Capra on Eastern Mysticism and Modern Physics', in *Science and Christian Belief* I, 1 (1989), p. 61, quoting also Davies and Brown (eds), *The Ghost in the Atom* (Cambridge University Press, 1986), pp. 54, 105 and 113

Rationality

One area of human life where it has often been claimed that some kind of discontinuity is called for is that of *reason*. The basic argument for this goes back, I understand, to Epicurus; it has been used in one form or another by philosophers as different as St Thomas Aquinas, J.M.E. McTaggart, and Sir Karl Popper. It was a favourite with the late C.S. Lewis, who used it for much the same purpose as I should like to use it – to establish the existence of a 'supernature' even in human life (in his case as a preliminary to defending the idea of the miraculous).

The argument has been given various forms. Let us begin with one by McTaggart,[1] directed in his case specifically against materialism: 'If materialism is true, all our thoughts are produced by purely material antecedents. These are quite blind, and are just as likely to produce falsehood as truth. We have thus no reason for believing any of our conclusions – including the truth of materialism, which is therefore a self-contradictory hypothesis.'

As it stands, this will not do. (In fairness to McTaggart, it should be added that it is only an extract from the syllabus of a lecture series, and was doubtless amplified in the lectures themselves.) It is open to two serious objections. Firstly, even if our thoughts are produced by purely material antecedents, are they really just as likely to produce falsehood as truth? How can the latter be inferred from the former? And secondly, even if they *are* just as likely to produce falsehood as truth, surely this does not show that materialism is false, but that we cannot prove that it, or anything else, is true. It could still be true, even if no-one knew it.

The second objection we can meet fairly easily. The argument, if valid, does not indeed show that materialism's truth is impossible; what it does show is that its truth is incompatible with the reliability of human reason. But we all rely on reasoning to some extent, materialists included, and, given a choice between abandoning all reasoning and abandoning materialism, most people would choose the latter. And, we might add, what McTaggart said of materialism seems to hold for any 'continuist' theory. For if any such theory is true, all our thoughts are produced by antecedents, not necessarily material ones, but certainly ones which existed before our reasoning began, indeed before our lives, or any human life at all, had begun.

These antecedents were wholly unconnected with my present thoughts (except as their causes) and thus are what McTaggart called 'blind'. They might lead to rational thoughts, but equally they might lead to irrational. If, then, our present thoughts can be *relied* upon to be rational, they are not wholly the product of antecedents which existed before our lives began, and in order to account for their reliability we must invoke some other factor, presumably a discontinuity. (We need not of course deny either that some thoughts may be unreliable; nor that our most reliable and rational thoughts are *partly* the product of remote antecedents. That I can think truly and reliably about Julius Caesar depends in part upon the events of Caesar's life, which was over long before mine began.)

It may be replied that continuism does not necessarily imply determinism. The laws which govern the universe may be – and the evidence is that lots of them *are* – statistical ones, which leave more than one possibility open in a given set of circumstances. As far as these laws are concerned, it may well be that in many cases the conclusions of my reasoning (or the physical events in my brain which correspond to those conclusions) are not entirely determined by the 'antecedents'. Now this is true enough; but can it make enough room for reliable rationality without abandoning continuism? I doubt it. For the Epicurus argument (if I may call it that) claims in effect that a rational mind must be able to act on the physical universe (via the brain and body): that is, that the physical universe is not a seamless web, not even an indeterminist one. Events in my brain which are unaffected by principles of rationality are as unreliable if they are 'chance' events as they would be if they were predetermined by the 'antecedents'. Indeterminism may be a necessary condition for rationality (indeed, I think it is); it is not a *sufficient* condition. And, we may add, the mind itself must be affected, not only by the past states of its 'closed inner unity', but by timeless truths of reason; but to this point we shall be reverting later on.

All this depends, naturally, on whether the Epicurus argument is valid. And is it? Professor A.G.N. Flew[2] treats it as a special case of what he calls the Conflict Thesis. This holds that what might be called 'mechanical explanations' (and mechanical questions, answers and concepts) are so different from *personal* explanations (questions, answers and concepts) as to be logically incompatible with them. The Epicurus argument is only a 'special case' of this, because the Conflict Thesis proper would hold that *any* explanation in personal terms – e.g. in terms of purpose, intention, wishes or the like – would be equally incompatible with mechanical explanation, whereas we are concerned only with explanations in terms of rationality.

But (Flew maintains) the Conflict Thesis is false. Consider a statement made by someone on a particular occasion. We may respond to it by considering its truth or falsity, and the reasons for holding it to be true or false, what Flew calls Subject Assessment. We may consider the making of the statement as an action, and look for its merits, motives, purposes, and so on, i.e. Action Assessment. Or we may consider the speaker simply as an organism and his or her utterances as 'so much acoustic disturbance'; the Physiological Approach. And there is, Flew claims, 'no fundamental inconsistency between any of these three approaches'; 'it is perfectly possible and proper to raise questions of all three sorts on and about one and the same occasion...That we can thus be simultaneously both rational beings, and moral agents, and living animal organisms, is one of the great basic facts about the multiple and complex nature of man.'[3] This is evidently meant as a demonstration of the falsity of the Conflict Thesis, though strictly speaking it is simply a *denial* of it, an assertion of the falsity without argument. Nevertheless, one's natural reaction is probably to agree with Flew. Surely there is no difficulty in treating this statement or utterance in all three ways? Do we not often do so? 'That is wrong, and you don't make it any more right by shouting it loud enough to be heard in Paris' would seem to include elements of all three treatments. And Flew has no difficulty in going on to show that some applications of the Conflict Thesis are quite incredible, such as the suggestion that a belief (a 'personal' concept) cannot be produced by a physical cause like drugs or brainwashing ('mechanistic' concepts). And if the Thesis leads to a false result, it is itself false.

But 'Epicureans' are not committed to the Conflict Thesis in its entirety. It is a far more extreme position than any they are likely to wish to take up. It is perfectly true that some 'personal' conditions can be caused by 'mechanistic' ones, that I may come to a belief or a desire as a result of physical events. Addicts of heroin desire further supplies of the drug, and believe that they need them, as a result of having taken the deadly substance in the first place – a physical event which may not even have been an action of their own, as one can be *born* an addict. The Conflict Thesis, then, cannot stand, not as a whole. But none of Flew's arguments or counter-examples (as opposed to his unargued claims) contradict the narrower thesis that there is a conflict between *explanations* in mechanistic terms and in terms of rationality. To the extent that we explain the addict's desire in terms of his or her physiology, to that extent we diminish or rule out explanation in terms of rational decision; we regard the addict as less than fully rational, and indeed less than a fully responsible moral agent. What is called for is a cure, not logical argument or moral exhortation. Again, consider Flew's own previous example of the making of a statement. The Physiological Approach, if it seeks to explain this event, points to occurrences in the lungs, larynx and mouth of the speaker;

before that, to occurrences in the nervous system; and possibly, if the Approacher is *very* ambitious, to the physical origins of that nervous system before birth. (In practice, of course, one cannot go so far back.) Now, are these occurrences necessary and sufficient conditions for the 'acoustic disturbance'? If not, then some other factor has to be brought in, which is precisely what the Epicurean or discontinuist maintains. But if they are both necessary and sufficient, how can the reasons the speaker had for believing and making the assertion, or the logical relationship between it and those reasons, *also* provide an explanation, or part of an explanation, for the making of it? Unless, indeed, the reasons and connections are actually identical with physical events, and I do not think even Flew would wish to maintain that. By saying that the mechanistic antecedents were sufficient by themselves to produce the event we call the making of the statement, we have denied that anything else contributed to it. Could it be that *either* set of conditions, mechanistic or personal, could have produced it on its own, but that by happy coincidence they worked in the same direction? Hardly convincing. Abandonment of the Conflict Thesis as a whole has not affected the Epicurus argument in the slightest.

Here, however, we can imagine an objector pointing out that there is certainly one class of events which *are* predetermined by physical antecedents and yet are also determined by logical relaionships. And since this is the case, there cannot be any incompatibility between the two sorts of explanation; there *must* be something wrong with the Epicurus argument. I refer of course to the results of computer calculations. If a computer is set to solve a particular equation, it does so according to physical laws which apply to its physical condition at the start of the computation; and yet its answer is intended to be the result of logical processes, whether or not we choose to call them 'thinking'. The double set of conditions, the physical ones and the logical, do apply in this case; why not also in the case of human beings?

This is plainly correct as far as it goes. It is in fact an instance of the one kind of case where there can be two sets of necessary and sufficient conditions: namely, where one set is itself a condition for the other. It may be a sufficient condition for my being overdrawn at my bank that I should have written cheques for more money than I have paid in; it may also be a sufficient condition that I should have developed habits of reckless extravagance. And if we eliminate certain other possibilities (e.g. that my excessive cheque-writing is simply the result of poor arithmetic) they may be necessary conditions as well. But of course in this case my habit of reckless extravagance is a necessary and sufficient condition of my overdraft *by way of* my excessive cheque-writing. A is the condition for B, and B the condition for C; and hence A is also the condition for C. There is no difficulty here. And the same holds good of our computer. It operates in accordance with physical laws, but these work on its original physical condition – the way in which it has been built and programmed in other words; and this was designed with logical processes in mind. A computer might be designed or programmed always to produce the wrong answer; it would be a pointless procedure, undoubtedly, but it would operate by exactly the same laws as a real, useful computer does. It is the design and programming of the computer which corresponds, in our banking analogy, to my habit of reckless extravagance; its operation in solving a particular problem, to my excessive writing of cheques; and the solution, to my overdraft. There is no conflict in either case; so does not Flew's contention hold good?

It is not enough to reply that the computer is unaware of its own rationality (or indeed its results). That is doubtless correct. But it is merely a repetition of the argument of our previous chapter, that consciousness breaks the pattern of continuity. We are trying to show here that reason does so too. And in any case a lot of the time we are ourselves unaware of our rationality or our reasoning processes. We suddenly 'come up with the answer', or 'see' the way to tackle the problem, without being aware of exactly how we did it, let alone whether the method used was logical.

But there are two other replies that are much better. One is to point out that the design of the computer was itself done with logical considerations in mind. The builders and programmers, as we have seen, could in theory have produced a totally irrational computation; that they did not do so is the result of rationality operating in *them*, and through them on their machine. We are brought back to our starting-point. How were their thoughts produced? By rational considerations, or by physical causes? If the latter, how can they also be relied upon to be rational thoughts? If the former, has not the Epicurean's point been conceded?

This pattern of reply looks likely to end in deadlock. The Epicurean says, 'Mechanistic conditions are incompatible with logical conditions.' The Continuist replies 'They are not – look at computers.' *Epicurean*: 'But mechanistic conditions for the *design* and *programming* of the computers are incompatible with logical conditions for them.' *Continuist*: 'They are not – there is no general incompatibility, as the computers show, so why should there be incompatibility in their designers?' Each side will seem to the other to be begging the question. To the Continuists, the Epicureans are trying to use their own belief – discontinuity – as a premiss to show that discontinuity is required for the design of the computer, when it is that belief that itself requires justification. But to the Epicureans, the Continuists are only showing that if discontinuity is not required for rational thought, it is not required for the rational design of computers, when it is that 'if' which they need to prove, and can't. I think that the Epicureans have the best of it, for it was their belief that held the field before computers were brought into the debate. But in any case there is another line that they could take.

The computer can be rational and mechanical at one and the same time because it has been designed to be. If it had not been so designed, it would be (in McTaggart's phrase) 'blind': mechanical, but not rational, even if it sometimes produced accurate results by sheer luck. But we, like the computer, are rational, and yet (it is alleged) part of a seamless web of physical nature. Did anyone design us?

A believer in the special creation of mankind by God will have no difficulty here. God made us rational beings (well, more or less rational), and we do quite often function as such. We are, so to speak, divinely designed computers. Of course, this lands us at once with a major theistic discontinuity. But perhaps God made the world in such a way that it was eventually bound to produce fairly rational beings? In that case, the discontinuity is pushed back into the act of Creation itself, which obviously is not part of the created world. Our problem is resolved. The solution may be an uncomfortable one for *atheist* continuists, but the present work is concerned with the theistic ones, who will not be disturbed at all. The Epicurean case is demolished.

And yet – is it? I am not sure. There are two difficulties, empirical rather than logical, which make me feel that the Epicurean may be right after all. One is the question of the *means* that God used to produce rationality. I suppose that most Christian continuists would assume that this was evolution by natural selection. (I am aware that there is some debate going on in scientific circles about the adequacy of this theory; but clearly it holds the field at present, and in any case if it were to be proved inadequate, the continuists' case will be worse off, not better.) But *could* natural selection produce rationality at the level at which it seems to exist in human beings? It is fascinating to realise that both authors of the famous paper at the Linnaean Society which started the evolutionary movement, Darwin and Wallace, thought that it could *not*, though they drew quite opposite conclusions from this. Darwin, discussing the whole question of belief in God, wrote 'I feel compelled to look to a First Cause...and I deserve to be called a Theist...But then arises the doubt, can the mind of man, which has, as I fully believe, been developed from a mind as low as that possessed by the lowest animals, be trusted when it draws such grand conclusions.'[4] In other words, the human brain is indeed the product of natural, 'mechanistic' causes, and cannot be trusted when it is trying to do work for which it was not selected by evolution. (One might wonder whether it can be trusted when trying to discover the process of the origin of species; but that is by the way.) Wallace, on the other hand, agreeing that natural selection could not produce a mind capable of these 'grand conclusions', and faced with the fact that grand conclusions are certainly drawn, not just in metaphysics, but in science, mathematics, and the like, concluded that something more than just natural selection was required. 'Natural selection could only have endowed savage man with a brain a little superior to that of an ape, whereas he actually possesses one very little inferior to that of a philosopher.'[5] To me, the interesting thing is that both were agreed that evolution by natural selection could not be the instrument, of God or chance, for the making of reliable human computers.

I am given to understand (just to confuse matters) that the most recent speculations on human evolution suggest that our mental development was not selected at all! We are seen as examples of 'neoteny', the preservation of juvenile characteristics into maturity. 'In particular', writes Professor R. Berry, 'our bones ossify much later relatively than apes, and this has the effect that our brains are comparatively much larger than in other primates. This has meant in turn an incidental effect of evolution in "releasing potential" for brain use...Human brain size and complexity were not selected for *per se*.'[6] And he compares this to the antlers of the Irish Elk, whose size caught up along with the increased size of the deer, but were not themselves the result of direct selection. Now if this is the case there is even less reason to suppose that evolution produced a brain that could be relied on to reason accurately in science or metaphysics. (The antlers of the Irish Elk were not intrinsically superior to other antlers!)

All this may yet be shown to be mistaken. But the Epicureans have one further move to make, I think; a move which does not depend on the state of evolutionary theory, and which might be a difficulty even for the Special Creationist. (I do not mean that it is an argument against special creation itself, only against a view, not in fact held as far as I know, which accepted special creation of the human race but denied discontinuity thereafter). Is it not the case that the logical or rational connection between propositions or beliefs is itself a causal factor in our acccepting them? This point is well put by Professor D.J. O'Connor,[7] and we may use his formulation the more confidently because he is not himself an 'Epicurean', and makes the point in the course of an argument *against* the Epicurean view. 'Consider', he says, 'what is involved in, say...the proof of a theorem in geometry. Once you have understood a particular step in the proof and seen that it follows from the previous steps in accordance with the rules of inference, you have no choice about assenting to its truth.' It is the words 'seen that it follows' that are the key point. If I see that a plate is cracked, the 'crackedness' of the plate is a causal factor in my seeing it. If I see that one step in the proof follows from the previous ones, surely the 'progression', that is, the logical relationship of implication between the step and its predecessors, is equally a causal factor in my 'seeing' of this, and hence in my assent to the validity of the proof. But this logical relationship is not a part of the physical world at all. O'Connor, granting this, argues that all this means is that 'it would certainly refute one type of determinism but only at the cost of conceding another. The causes that govern our assents will now be mental and not physical; but it is determinism for all that.'[8] But while my seeing the implication is certainly a mental event, the implication itself is *not*.[9] Sir Karl Popper has suggested speaking of three 'worlds', each affecting the others. 'World I' is the material cosmos, with atoms, cattle, stars and kettledrums. 'World II' is that of conscious experiences, thoughts, imaginings, and the like – what might loosely be called the 'mental' as opposed to the 'physical'. And 'World III' is the world of the objective contents of thoughts, of theoretical systems, critical arguments, and so on.[10] Now my recognising an implication is a mental event, part of 'World II'. But the implication is clearly part of 'World III'; if it affects my mental, and through that my physical life, neither of the latter is subject to determinism, whether mental or physical.

And it seems clear that there is a recognition of such a

relationship. In a computer, there can be – and normally is – a tendency to move from one step to the next that it implies. There could also no doubt be a kind of 'mechanical introspection' function by which the computer could record and report on its own workings. But it is hard to see how even in theory the computer could recognise 'implication' as such (though it could of course be programmed to use the word in printouts describing its own procedures). It can state that P implies Q; it can act on the basis that P implies Q; it cannot *recognise* that P implies Q. And we can. Which is why it can be programmed to do the first two.

Is this simply another repetition of the argument of the last chapter, that the computer cannot be aware of *anything*, and hence cannot be aware of a logical relationship? Not quite. For the computer can react to events and states of affairs in the world, even if it cannot be aware of them; they can, in theory, be immediate causes of changes within the computer. At least almost immediate; we must allow for such intermediate stages as light-rays, etc. And of course, in practice most computers use keyboards and other mechanical devices rather than literal visual scanning of the world around them, but this is not necessary to their functioning. It can react to the 'crackedness' of the plate, and would not react in the same way if it were not cracked. But if it is presented with the statements 'All men are mortal' and 'All Greeks are men', even though it may reply by printing 'All Greeks are mortal', it is to the symbols in which these propositions are presented that it reacts, in accordance with its instructions, not to the logical relationship between them. In so far as logical relationships enter into its activity at all, it is by way of construction and programming, not by way of information reception. That is to say, not only is it not aware of the relationships because it is not, properly speaking, aware of anything; even in the sense in which it is 'aware' of the symbols for 'All Greeks', etc., it is not aware of the 'World III' relationships between the propositions. And we are.

Popper, who began the terminology of 'Worlds I, II and III', argued further that in order to judge or describe the working of a computer (or a brain) we need to use World III language[11]. We need it for a standard of validity; otherwise we have no way of saying what it is that a defective computer or brain is falling short of. This is correct, no doubt; but I cannot see that it adds very much to the Epicurean case. Continuists will surely agree that validity is not a physical, World I property; their argument is simply that this is quite compatible with predetermination of all the workings of computers and brains by states and events that *are* in World I. (Popper seems to have had in mind an opponent who was a strict materialist, denying the existence of World III properties altogether; in that case his argument does have relevance, but there is no need to force materialism onto Continuists against their will.)

Is there any other way of avoiding a World III 'intrusion' into Worlds I and II? I can see only one, and it is so drastic that I think it will be unacceptable. Could it be simply that we learn by experience what patterns of reasoning lead from true premises to true conclusions? We could then apply the standards thus learnt to arguments for and against continuism, and conclude, it might be, that the former conformed more closely to patterns which work than the latter did.[12] In this case, we could avoid the idea of 'recognising validity' altogether; all we need is the power (not necessarily exercised consciously) to recognise when a pattern of reasoning has led to a true conclusion, and the power to draw the further, inductive conclusion that this pattern always, or nearly always, will lead to the truth (from true premises, that is). And it is conceivable, I suppose, that such powers might be developed as a result of evolution by natural selection. Unfortunately, such an argument involves abandoning not only the recognition of validity (which surely does occur, and ought *not* to be abandoned), but the whole concept of validity itself – indeed, the whole of deductive logic and mathematics. For it is an essential feature of these that they are unshakable by later experience, even in theory; whereas patterns learned to be reliable through experience may always be discovered to be less reliable than we thought, as our experience grows wider. We should be getting close to John

Stuart Mill's celebrated attempt to reduce logic and mathematics to generalisations about the world based on experience and corrigible by it, which has not as a rule been thought successful.

I am inclined therefore to believe that in reason we do have another case of discontinuity. But it would be as well to take note of one last reply that might be made by a continuist. Suppose that our thoughts are indeed affected by considerations of validity, implication and the like. Then, as O'Connor says, once you have seen that this step follows from the previous step, you have no choice about assenting to its truth. The causes of the assent are more varied than the materialist (or even O'Connor) realises: they include elements from 'Worlds II and III'; but surely there is continuity for all that?

Now O'Connor himself was criticising someone who wanted to see reasoning as an instance of *free will* in action; and against such a person he might perhaps be right. (I have my doubts even here; if I do not wish to assent to the last step, it is always open to me to backtrack and deny the truth of an earlier premiss. Besides, most of those who have used the 'Epicurean' argument have only sought to defend free will *indirectly*, by exposing a weakness in physical determinism.) But we are trying to consider reason as an instance of discontinuity in the physical world. And the fact that if the mental world is included continuity may be preserved does not affect the *discontinuity* in the physical world when taken on its own. There are irruptions into it from the mental level where we humans are concerned, and perhaps – we must decide this later on – where God is concerned as well. Moreover, as we have seen, recognition of logical relationships seems to entail discontinuity in the *mental* world as well. And it would, I think, be very hard to imagine some kind of continuism of three levels, with the mental level affected by Popper's 'World III', because the latter is surely timeless. It may not be completely impossible – the whole question of the relationships between the *timeless* and the temporal is a very complicated one – but I think it probably is. In any case, discontinuity on the two lower levels considered on their own would be established; and that is enough to be going on with.

Incidentally, the discontinuity involved in our reasoning (as with that involved in consciousness) suggests an *historical* discontinuity as well. There must have been a first creature or group of creatures to be 'aware' of its or their surroundings; there must also have been a first creature or group of creatures to realise the validity of a train of thought as well as simply being able to reason correctly. Many animals reason after a fashion, but I imagine that few if any ever recognise the accuracy of their own reasoning. We do both; and somewhere in the past there was a discontinuity, when first the idea of verity, correctness or validity dawned on someone – doubtless someone with no word for it and a sad problem over communicating his or her discovery to others. And a significant dawning it was, for on it depended huge structures of logic and mathematics and science, even perhaps a certain amount of theology.

Notes

1. *Philosophical Studies* (London, Arnold, 1934), p. 193
2. 'A Rational Animal', in Smythies, J.R. (ed.), *Brain and Mind* (London, Routledge, 1965), pp. 111 ff.
3. Art. cit., p. 117
4. *Life and Letters of Charles Darwin*, ed. Darwin, F., vol. 1, p. 282, quoted by Barbour, I., *Issues in Science and Religion* (London, SCM, 1966), p. 90
5. *Contributions to the Theory of Natural Selection*, p. 356, quoted by Barbour, op. cit., p. 92
6. Private communication, letter of 22 March 1982
7. *Free Will* (London, Macmillan, 1971), p. 44
8. Ibid.
9. There is indeed a theory that logical rules are purely human conventions; but, apart from many other difficulties, the

fact that certain theorems are entailed by these conventions is itself a logical truth and not a convention. Cf. e.g. Pap, op. cit., pp. 103-5

10. *Objective Knowledge* (Oxford, Clarendon Press, 1972), pp. 73-4, etc.

11. Popper, K.R., and Eccles, J., *The Self and its Brain* (Berlin, Springer, 1977), pp. 75 ff.

12. Cf. Campbell, K., in Edwards, P. (ed.), *Encyclopaedia of Philosophy* (London, Macmillan, 1967), vol. 5, p. 186 I think D. Hofstadter, *Metamagical Themas* (Harmondsworth, Viking, 1985), pp. 764-6, would *like* to say something like this, to provoke, but hesitates, concluding only that 'healthy logic is whatever remains after evolution's merciless pruning'.

Ethics

We may begin this section with two propositions which are quite indisputably true. First, that there are millions of living beings on this earth with a sense of good and evil, of right and wrong. Second, that at some point in the past, and at all times before that point, there were no living beings on this earth with any such sense. Where exactly the last point in time fell of which this second proposition is true, is not known, is not likely to be known, and does not matter. Somewhere, at some time, possibly at a number of places or times, an ethical or moral awareness came into being. And the discontinuity involved there and then was surely an enormous one, both in its nature and its effects.

Can we suppose that this change was simply a part of the evolutionary process? After all, there were points somewhere in the past when sight and hearing first appeared. Through some mutation, or rather some series of mutations, sensitivity to light and sound waves is thought to have come into being, and once they had done so their evolutionary advantages ensured that they would survive and spread, and (given help from further mutations) develop into full powers of sight and hearing. Could this not also have been the same with ethics? Sensitivity to good and evil is clearly of great help to a species which possesses it; it enables altruism and co-operation to exist, and so avoids a ferocious and destructive competition within the species.

Although this looks quite reasonable at first glance, there are two difficulties with it. One, which might perhaps be got round, is this: Co-operation and altruism are doubtless of genuine advantage to a social species of animal, such as ourselves. But they do not require an ethical sense to keep them in being. Bees co-operate admirably, to produce an elaborate and successful pattern of social life. They even display an element of altruism, defending the hive even though the act of stinging an enemy costs the individual bee her life. But there is no reason to suppose that bees have any sense of morality at all. Their patterns of behaviour are in themselves of value in preserving the species; they do not need any ethical foundation. Nor is there any particular reason to suppose anything different where (say) baboons are concerned rather than bees. They too co-operate to some extent, and they too show signs of altruistic behaviour; but as far as I know there is no evidence that they have consciences or a sense of obligation. Why then should natural selection favour a sense of right and wrong?

It could be objected that bees and baboons operate 'by instinct', whereas human beings have moved beyond the instinctive. (Which is no doubt true of bees at least; whether all baboon behaviour can be regarded as instinctive I do not know.) Since we have more to us than mere instinct, we need something more than instinct to regulate our behaviour. And this something is provided by the 'ethical sense'.

I am not sure about this argument. It may be correct. Some doubts are raised in me, though, by the fact that human beings *do* have instinctive behaviour patterns and, moreover, are quite capable of acting in a co-operative or altruistic fashion without being influenced by ethical considerations. A mother's care for her baby is not as a rule carefully thought out as part of her moral duty. It hardly occurs to most mothers *not* to look after the baby; and where the idea does occur to her sufficiently strongly to make neglect a fair possibility, a sense of duty is not very likely to call her back to caring. However, it could be that in so far as our conduct *is* thought out, and not unthinking or instinctive, it does require non-instinctive regulation, and that therefore once our species had evolved from pure instinct towards habits of thought, even to a limited extent, morality did become of value to it. So we shall not press this first argument against the idea of an 'evolved' ethical sense.

In any case, we do not *need* to press it, because there is a far stronger argument pointing to the same conclusion. This is as follows: sight and hearing are receptors of and responses to, natural physical phenomena, namely, light and sound waves. These waves existed before there were sentient beings on this planet; they affect and are affected by inanimate and non-sentient objects as well as sentient ones; the only difference introduced when creatures first began to see or hear was in the *way* this affected them. Consciousness, as we have seen, did introduce an new element into this; but even consciousness is and was of physical things and events. This is not the case with our awareness of good and evil. These are not physical things or events, nor are they physical qualities of things or events. Nor can we treat them as simply special instances of one of the discontinuities already discussed; they are not sensory qualities, nor are they part of reasoning (though of course we can reason *about* them). They form a category of their own. If it was a mutation that brought moral awareness into being, it was one wholly unlike those which brought sight and hearing into being; it was a far more serious breach in the continuity of the history of our race than those, for it brought us into contact with qualities which are real, but not part of the natural or physical world at all. (In this they resemble qualities like validity which we looked at above.)

There seem to be two possible ways to try and counter this argument. One is to claim that ethical qualities *are* part of the natural world (not necessarily physical – they might be mental qualities, or comprised of factors both mental and physical). For instance, it might be claimed that 'the conduct to which we apply the name "good" is the relatively more evolved conduct; and the "bad" is the name which we apply to conduct which is relatively less evolved.'[1] Or that 'good' conduct is that which satisfies the expectations of the society one lives in. Or that it is that which leads to the greatest pleasure for oneself, or the greatest happiness for mankind generally, and so on. In each case there is an attempt to define 'good', 'bad', etc., in terms which are not themselves ethical. And if this can be done, the discontinuity can be avoided; awareness of good and evil is awareness of something within the world, like awareness of dark and light.

Such proposals are certainly misguided. For good conduct surely consists of what one ought to do. This does seem to be a matter of definition, except possibly that there may be some acts of such goodness that 'ought' seems an inappropriate word to use of them. The life of St Francis was one of very great goodness, but it seems rather odd to say that he, or anyone else, *ought* to have lived the way he did. But then 'good conduct' also seems rather a feeble word to use of a life like Francis'. But it is not at all obvious that one always ought to follow the relatively evolved pattern of conduct, or do what society expects of one, or seek one's own pleasure, or even seek that of mankind generally. Even if it is in fact true that one of these is what one ought to do (the last is the most plausible candidate), it does not seem to be true simply in virtue of the meaning of the words. If somebody were to deny it – if, for instance, somebody were to claim that one should keep one's word even if greater happiness could be produced by breaking it – we cannot really answer 'What you say makes no sense. Ethical words like "should" are simply another, shorter way of referring to conduct which increases the general happiness. Your remark simply shows that you have not understood the meaning of the word.' If someone says that oaks are not trees, this does suggest that they do not understand the meaning of the word 'oak' or the word 'tree'; but not in our ethical case. The denier may be mistaken about the (ethical) facts; perhaps it would *not* be right to keep one's word in such circumstances; but the mistake would be over facts, not over language. And the only way to get round this is to use a definition of 'right', or 'good conduct', or whatever it is, which has a concealed ethical significance built into it: to define it, say, as 'conduct expected of one by the sensible elements of society' where 'sensible' means 'knowledgeable in matters of right and wrong'. And not only is this cheating, it fails to do what we set out to do, namely, understand ethical words in terms of natural qualities of some sort.

The other way out is to deny that in ethics we are brought into contact with real, objective qualities at all. This is, in various forms and with various qualifications, quite a popular doctrine among moral philosophers; but it is one that is likely to make a Christian, whatever his or her theological position, feel very uncomfortable. When we praise the Lord for His goodness, we are no doubt in most cases expressing our feelings or our adoration rather than stating a fact; and it is relevant that such praise is often expressed in the imperative mood ('Praise God, from whom all blessings flow') or the subjunctive ('Blessed be the Lord God of Israel') rather than the indicative. But when we state (or say, or think we are stating) that the Lord is good, surely we are doing more than expressing our feelings, or even our adoration (even though these probably enter into what we are doing); we are asserting something true about Him. Or so virtually all Christians would suppose, however radical their views in other respects. And of course it is not God alone to whom we should like to apply ethical terms. 'Good', 'righteous', 'sinful', 'upright', 'vicious', 'evil', 'holy' and the like are constantly occurring in Christian discourse and liturgy, and not least in the Scriptures themselves; and we usually suppose that the statements in which they occur really *are* statements, and are capable of being true or false.

The most plausible reply to this is that they do have some factual element, but that this is not ethical; and some ethical element, but that this is not factual. This comes out most clearly with words describing the specialised virtues (or vices). To say that Grace Darling acted bravely is to make a factual statement – she carried out very dangerous rescue work at great personal risk when most of us would have been too frightened or bewildered to do anything. But it is also to commend her actions. Whereas someone who said her behaviour was foolhardy would be basing this on exactly the same facts and passing a different judgment on them – a judgment which is not itself asserting any facts but those equally asserted by the 'bravely' version. (The latter is of course equally void of factual content as far as its commendatory side is concerned.)

Yet this is not altogether convincing. If (as is likely) most of us would wish to describe Grace Darling's behaviour as 'brave' rather than 'foolhardy', would we not feel that someone who did describe it as 'foolhardy' was not merely different from the rest of us but *wrong*? There is certainly a difference between us in our attitudes to her conduct, but it is not *merely* a difference in attitude, as there might be between supporters of rival cricket teams or between two people one of whom preferred orange marmalade and the other lemon. Moreover, there can be various grounds for commending or decrying something. I remember some years ago reading a condemnation of the South African government's apartheid policy in a satirical column in the *Daily Telegraph*; the writer condemned it as 'foolish'. Other people have also been known to condemn those policies, not because they were foolish, but because they were wicked, or unjust, or plain wrong. Now clearly there was no difference in attitudes here – both attitudes are of condemnation. Nor was there any disagreement over what the policies of the South African government actually were. The difference therefore was neither over non-moral facts, nor over general attitudes of commending and decrying: it is difficult not to conclude that there was a difference over *moral* facts.

The case for saying that there are no objective moral truths rests, I should imagine, on two bases.[2] Firstly, there is wide divergence over ethics between one society and another. Such practices as polygamy, human sacrifice, duelling, abortion and the charging of interest on loans have been regarded as legitimate, even right and proper, at some places and at some times; at others they have been regarded as very decidedly wrong. If we were aware of objective qualities of right and wrong, surely this ought not to happen. There is no disagreement between one society and another over (say) whether an elephant weighs more than a giraffe, or whether the sun gives light.

Of course, the reply to this is obvious. In most of these cases there is a disagreement over the non-ethical facts. Those who approve of abortion believe (on the whole) that a human life begins at birth; those who disapprove believe that there is no relevant difference between an unborn baby and a born one.

Those who approved of human sacrifice thought that the gods demanded it and would wreak a terrible vengeance if it were withheld; those who denounced it as wicked thought that no such demand had been made and no such results would follow. And so on. There is a very wide measure of agreement on certain very basic moral 'platitudes': that one ought to make people happy rather than miserable, tell the truth rather than lie, go gently with the weak, be loyal to friends and kindred – that sort of thing. There is nothing like such wide agreement on how these principles may best be put into effect.

Now this is a powerful reply, but not a complete one; and to show its incompleteness will lead us on to the second basis for denying the objectivity of ethics. Not *all* moral disagreements are over non-moral facts. Many more could more properly be described as disagreements over *weights*. You and I find that our friend X has been guilty of a moderately serious crime. We both feel the pull of loyalty and friendship; we both feel the pull of our obligations to society and the law (not to mention the victims of X's offence). But you, perhaps, give more weight to the former, and I to the latter. Is this compatible with the belief that we are dealing with objective truths?

It is, because the sort of situation described arises in many other contexts. In planning a holiday, seeking a job, deciding how to vote, we find ourselves weighing one consideration against another. (Deciding how to vote does no doubt have a moral side to it, but it is not the only side, and the same situation would arise even if only practical and selfish considerations were taken into account.) Yet whether we enjoy the holiday, make a success of the job, or benefit from the new Government are all objective facts. And though obviously we cannot tell for certain what would have been the result if we had gone on the other holiday, taken a different job, or voted for a different candidate, it is clearly objective facts that we are talking about when we speak of these possibilities, not something which is incapable of being true or false by its very nature. Otherwise we should have to suppose that it literally makes no difference what we decide! The logic of 'counterfactual conditionals' – '*if* P had happened (which it did not), Q would have followed' – is tricky, but the whole point of trying to work it out is to explain why some counterfactuals are true and others false. Now the weighing of considerations enters into such contexts as deciding whether it would be nicer to go to Wales or Norfolk next summer, and yet does not affect the objective truth of the statement 'Wales would be more enjoyable'. A small point of clarification here: You may prefer flat country to mountains, and I mountainous to flat; and so you may take the flatness of Norfolk as a point in its favour, and I the reverse. And there is presumably no objective superiority in either. But this is not a matter of weights. The mountains of Wales are not an advantage at all from your point of view; and that this is so is an objective fact. What matters is that we may assign different weights to factors we both agree to be advantages (or drawbacks) without this affecting the objective fact that one or the other holiday really would be the more enjoyed. Why then should the same 'weighing' process not enter into our decisions on moral questions without affecting the objective truth or falsity of the answers that we give to them?

This links up with another point that is sometimes made against the idea that ethical statements can be true or false. They are normative; that is, they are used to give advice, commands, or instructions. But can a fact advise, command or instruct? Surely when a fact is stated we are informed, not commanded or urged to do something. The function of ethical utterances is different from that of ordinary assertions, and there is no need to suppose that they express objective truth (or even falsity) in the way that ordinary assertions do.

True, in part anyway, but irrelevant. For ordinary assertions can be normative too – intended to produce or affect action, not simply convey knowledge. 'Help is on the way!' is intended to encourage holding fast till it arrives. 'It's a cobra!' is intended to produce a leap out of the way, or whatever action might be thought best to avoid getting bitten. 'Steep hill ahead' is meant to advise drivers to slow down. Our discussions about the places for a holiday, the potentialities of a job-opening, or the programmes of the political parties are all intended to affect actions, and yet need contain no ethical assertions whatever. And, conversely, ethical statements can be without normative intention; notably, those made about events in the past which are unlikely to be repeated in the experience of the hearer. To discuss, say, the rights and wrongs of the British Civil War of the seventeenth century is clearly possible, and yet the circumstances of that war are not likely to be repeated so that our ethical judgments about it can guide our actions now. It is more likely that our judgments about present political dilemmas will affect our conclusions about the Civil War.

It seems to me therefore that there is no good reason to doubt the objective truth of (some) ethical assertions, nor the fact that we can be aware of ethical truths; and if so, then we have here another and an important source of discontinuity in human life. But of course it is not just our awareness of such truth that really matters, it is the possibility that our lives are affected by this awareness. It does happen from time to time that we do something because we see it to be right, or refrain from doing something because we see it to be wrong. It does not happen nearly often enough, alas, but it does happen. And if I am right, then each time that it happens there is discontinuity at work; something that is more than earthly is touching our earthly lives, and the world is the better for its doing so.

Notes

1. Spencer, H., *Principles of Ethics* (London, Williams & Norgate, 1892-3), vol. 1, p. 25, cited by Flew, A., *Evolutionary Ethics* (London, Macmillan, 1967), p. 43

2. A third is sometimes added, what J.L. Mackie called the 'argument from queerness' (see his *Ethics*, Harmondsworth, Penguin, 1977, pp. 38 ff.): that moral perception, if it exists, is very unlike other modes of perception, and moral properties very unlike other properties. Since this is just what I am trying

to establish, I shall not try to counter it; only to say that to be different from other properties does not entail differing from them in objectivity.

Will

I turn now to a short section, yet perhaps the most crucial of all. Short, because the problems that are raised by discussion of the will are of great interest, complexity and difficulty, and to do them justice is so impossible that we may as well not try, and at least acquire the advantage of brevity. Crucial, because talk of divine action in the world is inextricably linked with talk about the divine will, and if the activities of the *human* will involve discontinuity in the universe, perhaps those of the divine may also. 'If the scientific view of the order of the world,' writes Peter Baelz, 'can make room for human freedom and human volition without disrupting its own procedures, so too can it, in principle, make room for divine freedom and divine volition.'[1]

We have in the preceding chapters seen that there is good reason to think that certain non-physical things, or non-physical properties of physical things, can affect the physical world. But this was always by way of human awareness: awareness in general (consciousness of the world about us), awareness of logical relationships, and awareness of moral truths or principles. Human *actions* did not enter into the matter, except in so far as they were caused by these states of awareness and provided evidence for them. Now actions certainly take place, and have effects. But do they too have a non-physical side to them?

Let us begin with a fairly traditional approach to the problem, which suggests an affirmative answer. Three people make statements. One says 'I have not tried to raise my arm, but it has gone up'. The second says 'I have raised my arm'. The third, who has, unwittingly, suffered a partial paralysis, says 'I have tried to raise my arm, but nothing has happened'. It would seem that the first and second have something in common – the movement of the arm – but that there is also something present in the second case which is *not* there in the first. And it looks as if this extra something *were* present in the third case, where the common factor of the first two (the going up of the arm) was missing. And this extra something, it is argued, is a mental event, an act of willing, a 'volition'. Here, then, it would seem, we have a non-physical act which has physical effects (except in the case of the paralytic), a discontinuity in the universe which derives from the human will.

Only, of course, it is not as simple as that. There are serious objections to the whole idea of an 'act of will'. Could it not be, for example, that the 'something' present in our third case which we supposed to be such an act was in reality one or more physical changes, which were not enough to lift the arm, but were enough to make the paralysed speaker aware of *something* going on? Perhaps a contraction of the muscles began, only not a sufficiently extensive one. It is very hard indeed to prove that this is not so: even if a particular suggestion about the supposed physical change should be ruled out, we cannot be sure that some other suggestion might not be able to do the job.

The nearest I can think of to a general refutation of this idea would be based on some celebrated experiments carried out by the Canadian neurosurgeon Penfield, in which he stimulated the brains of his patients in such a way that their hands moved. Surely, one might feel, all the bodily, physical mechanisms, in muscles and in the nervous system, which lead to the 'voluntary' movement of a hand, were present then? Yet the patients themselves denied that they had moved their hands. 'I didn't do it. You made me do it' was their reaction.[2] That is, the element common to our second and third speakers but not found in the first was not, it now seems, any of the physical events taking place between the brain and the hand. The only way out of this would be to claim: (*a*) that there is a physical difference between having cells in the brain cortex stimulated electrically by a neurosurgeon and having the same cells stimulated by the brain processes we call part of a voluntary action (which is no doubt true), (*b*) that this element of difference can be detected by the person involved and felt as the absence of volition, and (*c*) that this is what our third speaker was aware of in saying he or she had tried to raise an arm. Neither of these last two seems very likely. Incidentally, the difference is surely not that which the objector really needs. That would be the presence of a physical act of, or event within, the patient in normal circumstances which was missing in Penfield's experiment; the difference we actually have is the *presence* of the neurosurgeon's electrode.

A second objection would be one raised by J.F. Thomson in a broadcast symposium in the 1960s. 'Why', he asked, 'should we take it for granted that, whenever someone tries to do something, even if he fails, he always succeeds in doing something else, and that this is what his trying consists in?'[3] This surely has very little substance to it. In every other instance that I can think of, 'trying to do X' (whether successfully or not) does consist of doing something else which usually results, or which one hopes will result, in X's happening. I try to lift a weight by the muscular exertions which I believe or hope will make the weight rise. I try to get hold of an out-of-print book by looking in second-hand booksellers' shops, advertising, writing to possible sellers, and so on. It seems a counsel of despair to suggest that in just this one instance we have an example of trying which is *only* trying, all by itself, and cannot be analysed in the way all other cases can. Such a thing, neither an action, nor an event, nor indeed describable in any way except as 'trying', is hard to believe in, and seems to be distinguished from the equally non-physical[4] 'volition' only by an arbitrary fiat. (Although I used the expression 'act of willing' earlier on, it is by no means necessary to our present argument that this should be the correct description. All we need is a non-physical event, or circumstance, which normally leads to the raising of an arm, but in this case, because of the paralysis, did not.)

But the most celebrated attack on the idea of volition had come some years before Thomson and his fellow-symposiasts, in Gilbert Ryle's *The Concept of Mind*.[5] He raised four objections (apart, that is, from his criticism of the whole idea of the 'ghost in the machine'). The first is that we never actually talk about acts of willing in describing our lives (unless, that is, we are actually debating the question of whether there are such things). 'When a champion of the doctrine is himself asked how long ago he executed his last volition, or how many acts of will he executes in, say, reciting "Little Miss Muffet" backwards, he is apt to confess to finding difficulties in giving the answer.'[6] But of course exactly the same difficulties arise if one is asked when one last executed a *physical* act (or indeed 'an act' generally), or how many physical acts were involved in Ryle's unlikely recitation. Yet no-one doubts that there are such things as acts, and that reciting involves them. Our lives contain a multitude of physical acts, or, rather, a continuous stream of physical action, which cannot be divided up into discrete units except by *type*. That is, it makes no sense to ask when I last executed a physical act, though it does make sense to ask when I last stamped my left foot or potted a billiard-ball. Similarly, it makes sense to ask when I last chose to draw the curtains, and the answer is either 'When I last drew them' (unless perhaps it was an involuntary reflex!) or 'When I last tried to draw them but failed'. (In fact, of course, on the 'volition' theory an act like stamping the foot or drawing the curtains consists of a physical aspect and a mental one; except in peculiar cases like an involuntary movement or an unsuccessful attempt we have no need to treat the two aspects separately, and hence the fact that we don't talk about them in ordinary life is only to be expected.) Ryle appears to assume that if volitions occur at all, we should be constantly aware of them; but in fact life would be intolerable if we were. Nor of course are we aware of all our physical actions; in writing these sentences I was until a moment ago unaware of moving my pen across the paper. It is a commonplace that we are frequently only aware of a very general description of an action which is nevertheless a very complex whole. Driving a car, writing a letter or carrying on a conversation all involve a mass of actions and 'sub-actions' which never normally come to our full attention: if they did, our driving, writing or conversing would be seriously hampered. Might it not be much the same with our acts of will?

Secondly, (Ryle argued) we can never observe other people's volitions. We cannot therefore evaluate them for praise or blame. Thus, 'though volitions were called in to explain our appraisals of actions, this explanation is just what they fail to provide'.[7] And in so far as volitions were called in for this purpose, Ryle seems to me to have made his point. We appraise actions, or ascribe responsibilty for actions, by assuming that responsibility is there unless there is reason to think otherwise. And we judge that there *is* reason to think otherwise when we find that the 'act' was involuntary, or an accident, or done in ignorance or in fear of one's life; things like that. Some such excuses, one might add, apply even where volitions (if they exist) are present: the teller at the bank who hands over cash to an armed robber is generally excused, although if volitions exist the volition to hand over the cash was certainly present.

However, the wish to appraise actions is not the only incentive to belief in volitions or the will. As a matter of fact, in introducing the idea of volition in the present chapter, I made no mention of appraisals: only of the difference between raising my arm and my arm's going up. It is true that if there are such things as volitions, then their presence is doubtless a necessary (though not a sufficient) condition for the presence of responsibility; and it is also true that we cannot observe another person's volitions. But it is also true, if the physiologists are right, that certain events in the brain and nervous system are necessary (though not sufficient) conditions for the presence of responsibility; and yet we go on ascribing responsibility even in cases where the agent's brain and nervous system are not being monitored. So while responsibility does not provide evidence for volitions, neither does the fact that we can ascribe it (or refuse to do so) without reference to volitions provide evidence against them.

Ryle's third argument – and it is a favourite of nearly all critics of dualism – is the mysteriousness of the connection between volition and movement. 'The episodes supposed to constitute the careers of minds are assumed to have one sort of existence, while those constituting the careers of bodies have another sort; and no bridge-state is allowed.'[8] I must confess that I have never been able to see the force of this argument. The best reason we can ever have for believing that episodes of one kind can affect those of another (whether those episodes are physical, mental, financial or what you will) is evidence that they *do*. We may have other kinds of reason – prediction on the basis of scientific theory, for example, or divine revelation – but actual evidence is surely the best. And this, the dualist will say, is just what we have. We know that our feelings, anguishes, joys, reasonings, twinges of conscience and so on affect our bodily actions, whether they have 'different sorts of existence' from those actions or not. No doubt they usually affect those actions indirectly, but at some point the mental does affect the physical. It cannot therefore be an argument against volitions that they are mental and yet affect the physical. Ryle asserts that believers in volition have defined it as outside the causal system to which bodies belong; but surely it is he (or the tradition to which he adhered) who has tried to do this. Dualists have proclaimed all along that there is a *single* causal system to which body and mind both belong (though many have denied that it is a deterministic one). Of course, the possibility cannot be excluded that someone may prove somehow that the physical can only be affected by the physical; in that case it would indeed follow that the mental was not a separate 'sort of existence'. But a mere assertion is no proof.

Lastly, Ryle argued (and his argument was echoed in the symposium cited earlier) that the existence of volition is, supposedly, what allows outward acts to be 'voluntary, resolute, meritorious, and wicked'. But mental acts too can have these qualities. It follows that they too need volitions to start *them* off. But in that case volitions, being themselves mental acts, also require other volitions to start them off, and so on *ad infinitum* – unless they are involuntary, or perhaps neither voluntary nor involuntary. But in that case they cannot be resolute, meritorious, wicked or the like, which would surely embarrass moralists who think 'volitions' important.

That this argument is totally fallacious is easily seen by considering a parallel. It seems quite plausible to say that a shrewd manoeuvre by a general in battle must have been preceded by orders given by him. Otherwise it would hardly deserve the name of a manoeuvre at all – certainly not a shrewd one (nor even an idiotic). But the orders themselves could equally well be called shrewd. Must we then suppose that they were preceded by other orders, and these by others again, and so *ad infinitum*? Clearly not: yet on Ryle's argument it would seem that they had to be – or else that orders are after all unnecessary for manoeuvres. All this is absurd; and so is the parallel argument against acts of the will.

I think that if I did want to criticise the old-fashioned idea of volitions, it would be on the grounds that while there certainly is something mental accompanying and causing bodily actions, it does not consist – not as a rule, anyway – of discrete acts of the will. (This is the valid point contained in Ryle's first argument.) 'We are apt', noted C.A. Campbell, 'to think of volition in terms of the deliberate choice between alternatives, which is of course *not* an activity that is pervasive of normal waking experience. But deliberate choice between alternatives is only one particular species of volition. The *genus* is the self's identification of itself with a conceived end: and this, though present in very varying degrees of explicitness, it is not paradoxical to regard as "pervasive of normal waking experience"'.[9] We might quote here, too, some remarks of William James. James suggested that most 'voluntary' movements have no 'fiat, mandate or express consent'. They follow simply upon the idea of the movement. If (to take James' example) I notice dust on my sleeve while talking, I brush the dust off without interrupting the conversation, and without any explicit decision to do so: 'the mere perception of the object and the fleeting notion of the act seem of themselves to bring the later about.'[10] Yet clearly such an act is in some sense a voluntary one; it is not like walking downstairs while looking at the wallpaper, when one's feet seem to carry one down of their own accord. Given that the perception and the act are not quite enough to cause the act –

the notion seems to come with a flavour of assent which may be Campbell's 'identification with a conceived end' – these accounts seem to be fairly similar, to one another and to what one normally experiences.

Of course, the existence of what we may call volitional activity does not rule out continuism of all kinds. It could still be that the will itself was governed by laws (psychological ones, presumably); and it might even be thought that the will was no more than 'froth on the wave of physical reality'.[11] The latter can easily be disproved, or at least rendered virtually incredible. As we have seen, it is quite certain that mental events or qualities do have effects on the physical world. If they did not, we should be unable to discuss them (since discussions are part of the physical world, though of course *more* than just that): or, alternatively, we should be discussing them as if they affected it, and in exactly the same words as we should if they did, even though in fact they did not. The first of these alternatives is false, and the second is unbelievable. We cannot, I suppose, rule out the possibility that while sensations, emotions and imaginations affect the world, the one aspect of the mind that does not is the will *to* affect it; but somehow this does not sound very convincing.

As for the former suggestion, the possibility that the will behaves without discontinuity, being governed by psychological laws, if those laws reduce in the end to physical ones, as Freud, for instance, believed, we are in effect back to the 'froth on the wave' fallacy. But suppose they are not thought of as physical, even in the long run; suppose they are thought of as genuine, irreducible laws governing the behaviour of the will? In that case (*a*) there is still discontinuity in the physical world considered by itself, since mental qualities or events affect it, and in the mental world considered by itself, since physical qualities and events affect *it*. Still, it might be that there was continuity in the two considered together, however unlike the normal scientifically-minded continuist's picture of things this might be; so we do not yet have a conclusive argument. (*b*) The laws have not yet been discovered, not even in first approximations.[12] The best we can deliver are rough generalisations, themselves often bitterly disputed (as with those proposed by the psychoanalysts), or statistical laws governing the behaviour of large numbers of people, and even these seem to change. (The economic 'laws', for instance, propounded by Adam Smith or Karl Marx, applied quite well to their own times but hardly at all to, say, ancient Greece – or the world of today.) And these statistical laws are simply statements of prevalent patterns among chains of events which may well be wholly discontinuous in their nature. (*c*) There are very strong reasons for thinking that our wills are to some extent not predetermined but free: notably the argument that it is not possible to say (truthfully) that X ought to have done Y unless he or she *could* have done Y; that if X's will was predetermined to do, not Y, but Z, by causes not under his or her control, X could not have done Y; and that therefore if X's will was predetermined (which on the theory we are considering is always the case), it is never possible to say truthfully that X ought to have done Y in cases where he or she did not in fact do it. But that we *can* truthfully say such things in innumerable actual cases is far, far more certain than any of the arguments for psychological laws governing all the life of our will.

A great deal more can be said on the freedom of the will: a great deal more *has* been said, by both determinists and indeterminists, and in my opinion the indeterminists have had the best of it, though it is only fair to say that the majority opinion among philosophers is probably the reverse. But if mental events or qualities can be shown to have physical effects, and if good reasons can be given for denying that they are themselves determined by psychological laws, the remainder of the 'free will debate', fascinating though it is, may be passed over here. We have, on a miniature scale, something analogous to what traditional theism has believed about God: there is a world which operates most of the time according to its (God-given) laws and principles, but which a mind can, and sometimes does, affect in a way which either goes contrary to those laws or is not predetermined by them (because they are themselves not deterministic but statistical, and do not 'lay down' anything for individual events).

CREATIVITY AND IMAGINATION

Human creativity, and in particular the creativity of the artist, is often taken as the most obvious example of all of the introduction of something new into the world. Even the child at the seashore making castles and canals with bucket and spade seems to be bringing a new thing into existence: how much more a Giotto, a Shakespeare, a Mozart? Similarly with the scientist: the lives of Newton, Darwin and Einstein produced notable discontinuities in the history of the world. So for that matter did that of Marx – and that of Jesus. Civilisation is built on such discontinuities; it thrives by converting them into something that endures, weaving their consequences into the continuity that previously existed: without this we should still be in caves (if indeed we had ever got as far as entering them).

Of course the continuist's answer is obvious enough. These are only *apparent* discontinuities. The sandcastle is in fact composed of grains of sand that were there already, dampened by a sea that was there already too. Even the thoughts of the child who made it were shaped by previous events – by the seeing of real castles and canals, or pictures of them, or by the suggestions of parents who had played on the beach in their own childhoods, and so on. What appears to us to be entirely new is simply the rearrangement of pre-existing material in a pattern which was always possible, even if it had never happened in just that way before. Weathering may shape a rock into the likeness of a camel; I have seen an instance. But no-one supposes that anything other than natural, continuous processes were at work in such a case. Why should we suppose this simply because the processes operated by way of the hands and brain of a child? The child may not be aware of being part of the same process as the waves or the sand in the 'creation' of his or her castle and canals, but that is in fact what the truth of the matter is.

Well, maybe so. But even if this has some plausibility in the case of a comparatively trivial 'creation' like that of the sandcastle, does it have the same plausibility when we come to major achievements of the human mind and spirit? Obviously it can in theory be maintained; but can it really be believed? It was the famous contention of Laplace (and the supreme expression of continuism) that 'an intelligence which, for a given instant, knew all the forces animating nature and the location of the various objects that comprise her, and which was moreover so vast that it could put all this material under analysis, could grasp in a single formula the motions of the largest bodies in the universe and those of the lightest atom; for it, nothing would be uncertain, and the future, like the past, would be present to its eyes.'[13] But all the creative work of the human race is embodied in physical results – books, speeches, manuscripts, songs, sculptures, paintings, scientific treatises, and the like. The 'intelligence', therefore, could predict all future and 'retrodict' all past creative work; it might have no *appreciation* whatever of its true nature, but it could calculate it. The consequences of this have been pointed out very forcibly by Popper:

> If physical determinism is right, then a physicist who is completely deaf and who has never heard any music could write all the symphonies and concertos written by Mozart or Beethoven, by the simple method of studying the precise physical states of their bodies and predicting where they would put down black marks on their lined paper. And our deaf physicist could do even more: by studying Mozart's or Beethoven's bodies with sufficient care he could write scores which were never actually written by Mozart or Beethoven, but which they would have written had certain external circumstances of their lives been different.[14]

(Incidentally, the physicist could also have written Popper's lecture for him; but this Popper modestly concedes to be a lesser achievement.)

Of course, this 'deaf physicist' is a wild exaggeration. Not the most brilliant physicist imaginable could do the calculations envisaged (or get the necessary information together). But Laplace's 'vast intelligence' could, in theory, do both, while being just as uncomprehending in all matters of music as Popper's deaf physicist. Or could it? Since Laplace's day a strong element of indeterminism has crept into physics. The Intelligence could not acquire all the data that Laplace's idea requires; and if it could, still the laws of physics are only statistical, and do not demand that events be wholly determined by their predecessors. Not even the Intelligence could predict a Mozart symphony if non-determined events contributed crucially to its composition.

But this will hardly answer Popper's protest. For while it does show that our unmusical Intelligence might not be able to predict the symphony, this is not because the Intelligence is unmusical, or because Mozart was a rare and wonderful genius; it would be hampered in exactly the same way in attempting to predict when a given atom of uranium would begin to decay. It is not the creativity of Mozart or Beethoven that means a tone-deaf Intelligence could not write their music for them; it is only the fact (if it is a fact) that sub-microscopic events in their brains were involved in the process of composition. I think that continuists would do better simply to accept the challenge head-on and say that 'creativity' simply *is* a product of predetermined forces plus an element of sheer chance. I shall not believe them; but I do not see how they can actually be refuted.

Creativity, however, is not (despite what was assumed at an earlier stage) limited to marks on paper and canvas or shapes in sand and bronze: the composer or artist – perhaps even the child with the bucket and spade – may well first have 'created' visual or auditory images in his or her mind. (Ryle showed quite clearly that this *need* not be so; but in some cases it certainly is.) Most of us, even the inartistic, have done so from time to time, though the extent to which mental images play a part in one's thinking varies greatly from one person to another. But there is something very odd about mental images. They come into existence out of nothing. At one time I may have no such images at all; a few moments later I may have a varied and vivid set of them. They are not physical objects; they are not constituted by changes in a physical object (my brain) even if they are *caused* by such. Nor are they constituted by changes in other mental images – or rather, the first ones to appear in a given sequence of images are not; for, as we have seen, they may come after a time in which no images at all were present. Their arrival in the mind is an example of serious discontinuity; it is perhaps the closest we get to that creation *ex nihilo* by which God causes a world to be. Not even the Laplacean 'Intelligence' could predict their existence, as they are not objects within the physical universe, not even its 'lightest atoms', and are mentioned therefore neither in the Intelligence's data nor in its catalogue of forces. And of course if such images, auditory ones in this case, played a causal part in the composition of, say, a Mozart opera, the continuist's position would be not just incredible but untenable too. However, in fairness, one should add that it might be difficult to prove this. Perhaps Mozart had no mental images of the sounds he was creating. (It would be easier to make the point with Beethoven after his deafness began.) Or perhaps he had them, but they were mere epiphenomena, which contributed nothing to the actual composition. (Of course, reports of his mental imagery, or anyone else's, would be another matter. These are events in the physical world which are undoubtedly caused in part by non-mental events in the images themselves. We have already come across this point in our discussion of consciousness.)

It is, surely, a fair conclusion that in artistic and other forms of creativity we have instances of novelty and discontinuity within the physical world which it is not possible to explain convincingly as entirely the products of other factors within that world; in the imagination we have novelty and discontinuity in a non-physical part of God's creation which themselves may help to produce the physical discontinuities of the first type.

Notes

1. Baelz, P.R., *Prayer and Providence* (London, SCM, 1968), p. 113

2. In Farber, S. and Wilson, R., *Control of the Mind* (New York, 1961), cited by Koestler, A., *The Ghost in the Machine* (pbk, London, Pan, 1975), p. 203

3. In Pears, D. (ed.), *Freedom and the Will* (London, Macmillan, 1963), p. 21

4. To be fair, Thomson would probably have denied that 'trying' could be called a non-physical event or state of affairs. Indeed, he had just raised our previous point about there being perhaps some physical event that our second and third cases had in common.

5. London, Hutchinson, 1949

6. Op. cit., p. 65

7. Op. cit., p. 66

8. Ibid.

9. *On Selfhood and Godhood* (London, Allen & Unwin, 1957), p. 148

10. *Psychology (Briefer Course)* (New York, Collier, repr. 1962), p. 421

11. The phrase is J. Searle's ('Minds, Brains and Science', i, the *Listener*, vol. 112, no. 2883, 8 Nov. 1984), p. 15. The phrase does not describe Searle's own view.

12. This applies even more strongly to the theoretical possibility that mental events and qualities, though having physical effects, are themselves entirely determined by their physical antecedents. I do not think anyone has ever actually held this position, which involves the odd consequence that thoughts, etc., may produce bodily actions but never other thoughts.

13. 'Théorie Analytique des probabilités', quoted by Babbage, C., *Ninth Bridgewater Treatise* (London, Murray, 1837), note C, pp. 173-4

14. *Objective Knowledge* (Oxford University Press, rev. edn, 1979), p. 223

Religion

Our question here is, can an account of religion be given which does not involve any kind of special causal link between the normal world and God? Naturally, the atheist will have to answer 'Yes', and try to give a purely naturalistic account of religion. Many widely differing attempts have been made to do just that: it arose from some sort of universal Œdipus complex, or out of the failure of magic to work properly, or out of a projection of our own inner being, or out of the sighs of the oppressed – out of practically anything except an apprehension of reality. Fair enough; if we know in advance that the thing cannot be true, there must be some explanation for it. But we are concerned in the present essay with those who do not believe all religion untrue, with people who wish to understand the world in a religious way, more specifically in a *Christian* way. Is it possible for *them* to give an account of religion which does not entail serious discontinuity in the universe?

In so far as religion is a human activity, like athletics, learning Spanish, or coal-mining, of course such an account can be given. (An account; not necessarily an explanation!) Sociologists, historians and psychologists are all willing to do so. And it is possible to describe religion in this sort of way while at the same time believing the world to be the creation of the Christian God. There are, after all, Christian sociologists, historians and psychologists. It is when we try to link these accounts and the belief in God, to see how they relate to one another, that the trouble begins. Are we to suppose that it is simply coincidence that the religious believer holds opinions about the world, and takes an attitude to it, that are substantially correct? That seems a little unlikely, but the alternative is to suppose that these attitudes and beliefs are not explained by the accounts we have given of them, only described. They are apparently justified as well as correct. And how (on the continuist hypothesis) can such justification be possible?

Christians (and many others) have usually held that their beliefs were justified by the fact that they were rooted in God's revelation. He had revealed, through prophets, sages and saints, that He was One, just, loving, almighty, and unchanging; He had revealed the depths of His love by becoming man and dying for us. There might be discussion and debate about the exact nature of this revelation to us (we shall have more to say about this later on), but hardly on the *fact* of it. Such a position, however, is impossible for the continuist. If God does not act through chosen events in the world, He does not use such acts to reveal Himself to us. And without such acts it is difficult to see how revelation would be possible. If a supposed revelation were part of the 'seamless web', it would be determined by preceding conditions just like any other event, and these in turn by the conditions that preceded *them*, and so on; the supposed revelation would have no connection with the God who was supposed to have revealed it, or whom it was supposed to reveal, which it did not share with every other state of affairs in the universe. And remember, those other circumstances include all false 'revelations'. There would be no distinction between the words of Jesus and the words of Joanna Southcott. Both would be the result of causes operating within the universe; both would be equally the work of God; if we wanted to distinguish between them, to decide which one told the truth, it would have to be without regard to their origin.

It might be argued that in any evaluation we have to use some basis other than that of origin to decide between alleged revelations, because we can only see the earthly, human end of the revelation. The words of Jesus, or Hosea, or Joanna Southcott, these we can be aware of; their alleged source in the mind of God, that is inaccessible. Therefore if we choose to believe Jesus or Hosea, it is not because their words came from

70 The New Deism

God; we believe that they came from God because we believe them to be true. And we do this, perhaps, because of the wisdom and holiness of their authors and their contents, or the like. And this is something we are able to do whether we are continuists or discontinuists.

There is some force in this, but not very much. It is quite correct to say that Jesus or Hosea could be telling the truth whether or not they were specially inspired by God in a direct way. It is quite correct to say that we believe in the truth of their revelations without having access to the mind of God. But in the first place, one major reason for believing in their truth is that they appear to be part of a continuing and generally consistent process of revelation from Abraham onwards; on the continuist hypothesis they are not. They do not support one another so that their agreements might bear them out and suggest they came from the same source. Nor does their membership of the same series of prophetic 'revelations' mean that the appearance of truth in one suggests probable truth in the other. On the contrary, when they agree, it is presumably often due to un-thinking acceptance of a common background of thought; their membership of the same series is only of historical interest; and their agreement, being historically based, is if anything a very slight reason for *hesitation* in believing them, by reducing the role played by their individual wisdoms.

In the second place, these people made certain claims about being vehicles of revelation. They supposed that they had seen the Lord, or heard His voice in their hearts, or been sent by Him with a mission to the world. If God does act in the world, by granting visions, speaking to hearts, or sending people on missions, then some who make such claims may be speaking the truth. But if He does not, they were all grievously mistaken or deplorably untruthful. We have therefore strong reason to disbelieve a crucial point in their proclamation and this seriously reduces the credibility of the rest of it. If Jesus, or Hosea (or Muhammad, or Guru Nanak) so seriously misunderstood or misrepresented the facts about God in this particular area, one naturally wonders whether they may not have misunderstood or misrepresented other facts about Him as well.

It may be objected, as we shall see later on, that it is a mistake to assimilate all revelation on the prophetic model. Other forms of revelation exist: side by side with Isaiah and Amos stand the Psalms and the Proverbs. What of revelation through the medium of Wisdom? Cannot God grant people wisdom and insight into spiritual areas without the direct contact with their minds which was claimed by the prophets?

Undoubtedly He can, and I am sure He has actually done so. But the granting of wisdom and insight is as much an interference with the continuity of the world as the giving of a prophetic message. Unless, that is, the wisdom or insight was given indirectly, through the normal processes of nature, the wisdom of (say) Solomon being the product of his genes and his environment, much as his height and weight were. And in that case we run up against a difficulty. Why should we believe Solomon? When he spoke of trees and birds, reptiles and fish, it was doubtless possible to check what he said, and confirm that he was indeed wise. But when he spoke of God and things beyond the circles of this world, no such check could be made. Of course, if these supernatural realities could themselves be the direct cause (or partial cause) of what he said, in the way the birds and trees were, then we might be justified in inferring from his proven wisdom in earthly matters that he was also wise in heavenly ones. But on the continuist hypothesis the supernatural realities were *not* part of the cause of his proverbs about them (except in so far as God is the cause of all things, including both the wisdom of Solomon and the folly of Nabal). 'Wisdom' is no more reliable for justifying a continuist's religious beliefs than 'prophecy'.

It is not therefore open to continuists to believe that religion can originate in divine revelation, or be justified by appeal to it. Can they, then, adduce 'religious experience' as its true origin or justification? This is certainly the line taken by Professor Wiles. 'What kind of affirmation about God', he asks, 'does Christian experience justify?'[1] And the answer (on his own hypothesis) is of course quite simple: none at all. There can be no experience of anything except an event or state of affairs within the world. Undoubtedly, if the world was created by God, Christian experiences are ultimately the effect of God's creative will; but so are all other experiences. The Christian's profoundest moments afford no better reason for affirming anything about God than the experience of feeling cold or seeing a wombat. The only difference is that in so far as they appear to imply contact with One who is not part of the created world they are delusory and misleading, which is not true of feeling cold or seeing wombats.

Of course, not all 'religious experience' is supposed to be a direct awareness of God. 'Part of the experience of God is experience of that which makes ultimate sense of things', writes Professor Wiles,[2] 'not only in terms of their being there at all but in terms of an overall and ultimate purposiveness in them.' Now this looks a good deal more hopeful for the continuist. For the 'things' which have an overall and ultimate purposiveness about them are things within the world, and there is no discontinuity involved in our awareness of them and of their properties, which presumably include the property of purposiveness. Or is there? If we *infer* their purposiveness, no, although reason itself may involve discontinuity, as we have seen. If I observe a general direction of events – towards a maintenance of order and stability, or towards the 'heat-death of the universe', or whatever it may be – and infer from this a purposiveness behind the direction, then, whatever the validity of my inference, there is no breach in continuity. But I have not in this case *experienced* 'that which makes ultimate sense of things'. I have reasoned my way to belief in it. If, however, it is claimed that one can experience the purpose itself, then, the purpose being a property of the mind of God, it is not something within the created universe, and the continuity is broken after all. Unless, indeed, one can somehow experience purposiveness (as opposed to mere direction) in things without being aware of the purpose which guides them, which seems unlikely. Once again the appeal to religious experience has failed to justify religion – *unless* that experience is of something outside the created universe, in which case its continuity is not complete.

Bultmann's approach was somewhat different. In 'mythological thinking', he argued,[3] the action of God (whether in nature, history, human fortune, or the inner life of the soul), the divine causality, was thought of as being 'inserted as a link in the chain of events which follow one another according to the causal nexus': the sort of thing which we have been calling a special divine act, or an intervention. Bultmann, of course, did not believe in such. But he was faced with the objection that Christian preaching must speak of God as acting; does this not mean that Christian preaching must therefore be 'mythological'? 'No,' he replied: 'for the action of God is unworldly and transcendental; it must be thought of, not as happening *between* the worldly actions or events, but as happening *within* them.' 'If someone now insists that to speak in this sense of God as acting is to speak mythologically, I have no objection', he continued, 'since in this case myth is something different from what it is as the object of de-mythologizing.'[4] One is rather tempted to agree: to say that as the object of 'demythologising' the 'myth' of God's acting was at least intelligible, whether it was true or false, whereas in Bultmann's sense it is meaningless verbiage. What the sense might be of 'action' which leaves the connection between natural and historical events intact (i.e. they would be exactly the same whether God acted 'within' them or not), and what the sense of this metaphor of 'within' can be, are both profoundly obscure. Such a reaction would not perhaps be completely fair, for Bultmann did allow that in speaking of God as acting we conceive His action as an analogue to actions taking place among people; 'it is in this analogical sense that we speak of God's love and care for men, of His demands and His wrath, of His promise and grace.'[5] This is better; but it will not really do what Bultmann evidently wants it to do: make sense of his metaphor and his idea of God's action. God's action is analogous to human action, not exactly like it? But is this not because God is very different from us? Is not the difference on the part of the agent? For Bultmann to make any use of this idea of analogy, however, the difference must lie in the result as well as in the agent. If I act on a chain of events – if, let us say, I try to reconcile two friends who have quarrelled – I insert a new event, my soothing words, into the chain, and make the later events in it other than what they would have been if I had not acted. And this is exactly what Bultmann wants to deny happens when God 'acts'. If God meets us in His Word, as assuredly He does, does this meeting make a difference in my life, make it other than what it would have been if the words had been the same but the Lord had not been in the words? If the answer is 'Yes', then the causal nexus has been interrupted; if the answer is 'No', then we reduce 'God's action', and the faith to which it leads, to psychological events produced by purely natural means, and add nothing whatever to a description that leaves 'God' out altogether.

It may be felt that in treating of Bultmann at all under the heading of 'justifying' religion we have done him an injustice. Surely he himself would have rejected the whole idea of trying to justify faith? God's actions are and must be hidden. And this is no doubt correct. There are serious and well-known objections to such an attitude (notably, how does one then react when confronted with somebody who takes the same attitude, only with a different faith?); but this is not the place to go into them. I introduced Bultmann really because if he had been right, if there had been an intelligible sense in which God could have been spoken of as acting within events rather than upon them, then the faith aroused by such actions would have been in theory justified, even if in practice we could not prove its rightness, whether to ourselves or to anyone else. We should have shared the believer's predicament over the question of verbal inspiration of the Bible. If God did in effect dictate the Bible, then reliance on it would make sense, even if we were unable to prove that He had in fact dictated it rather than the Koran. Similarly, if God could intelligibly be said to meet us in His Word in a continuist framework of speech and thought, faith and religion would be in reality justified, even if we were unable to prove that justification. Unfortunately, the thing cannot be said. If the Word in which God is supposed to meet us, and the effects it has upon us, are all part of the causal nexus, there is not, even in theory, any justification for those effects, whether they are faith or boredom. If faith is the more appropriate reaction to the preaching of the Church, this is just a coincidence.

Much the same holds with other forms of experience. Many people have been led to faith by the experience of 'conversion'. Well and good. But if this conversion is the direct work of God the Holy Spirit, it is a breach of continuity; if it is not, then it is presumably explicable in natural terms, and is no justification for the faith to which it led. Many, again, have spoken of the experience of the 'numinous', of a *mysterium tremendum et fascinans*. If this is awareness of a mysterious, awesome and fascinating quality in things of this world, it is interesting no doubt but of no value for affirming anything about God or the divine; if it is an awareness of something not part of the created world, it is of great value – to the discontinuist. In sum, no experience can be any evidence for the truth of a religion unless we admit discontinuity; for the experience, being part of the 'seamless web spun upon the loom of time', would have occurred just the same had the religion been false.

If, therefore, Christianity (of however attenuated a kind) cannot, on the continuist hypothesis, be justified by appeal either to divine revelation or to religious experience, only one possibility seems to remain for continuists. They must stake all on natural theology, or else admit that their position is irrational and unjustifiable. Yet as a matter of fact, few if any present-day continuists are avowed supporters of natural theology. (In this they differ very notably from their eighteenth-century deist predecessors, and differ for the worse.) Professor Wiles does speak with some courtesy of the cosmological argument, in the passage cited just now, but he regards it as invalid as an inference; its strength lies, he believes, in a covert appeal to our sense of wonder that anything should exist at all. But a sense of wonder is of psychological rather than theological interest. If we are *right* to feel wonder at the fact that anything at all exists, we are on the way to an actual argument; but if the argument is invalid, the wonder is of no weight. If the cosmological argument is valid, the wonder may reflect a dim, inarticulate awareness of its validity; if it is not, and yet discontinuity exists, the wonder may reflect a dim awareness of the God who created all things; but if the argument is invalid and there is no discontinuity in the world, this sense of wonder will take us no nearer to a justification of belief than we were without it.

Now I am myself far from regarding natural theology as useless: I do think that some forms of the cosmological and physico-theological arguments have great, though not inescapable, force; and I am inclined, though much less confidently, to think that Kant's form of the moral argument may have some force as well.[6] But even with all this we are a long way from the God of Christian continuism, let alone from the God of the Bible. Suppose that the two classical arguments are valid: then we know that there is a First Cause of the universe, and a source of the order within it. But whether this Being loves us, or deserves our worship and reverence, this we do not know. If the Kantian argument is also valid, we know also that He, She or It is a power working for good. That is a major step forwards, but it still says nothing about any kind of personality in this Being, let alone any possibility of a personal relationship with it, in faith, love, adoration, prayer or the like. And I feel sure that the Christian coninuists do desire some such relationship and believe it a possibility. But even if it is a possibility, it is a possibility of which, on their principles, we can never know.

It is not so with the rest of us. If the natural theologians are right in assuring us of a Source of existence, order and justice, we who feel able to believe in the Christian revelation can point out to them that One who claims to be that Source has spoken through prophets, apostles, sages and evangelists, and, supremely, through His Son; we who feel able to believe in real religious experience of that which is beyond this world can also believe that this Source and Revealer can be met, known and loved as our Lord and our Saviour. The divine interventions bear out and give content to the thin and skeletal evidence of natural theology, which would by itself be of little or no value, except to the curiosity of the intellect.

I will add one last point. Suppose that the natural theologians are right, and that religion can be justified to a certain extent by reason. Now natural theology seems to begin, in the Western tradition, with Plato; it also appeared in India, but only rather later. It follows that not until then (indeed, possibly not until valid formulations of the theistic arguments were devised) was religion more than unjustified guesswork. Jesus' attitude to his 'Father' had no basis whatever; he may, by a lucky chance, have hit on something fairly close to the truth, but that is the most we can say, for there is no reason to suppose that he was affected, even indirectly, by the natural theology of the philosophers. Certainly Moses, Isaiah and the rest were not; their dates preclude it. Theism, widespread though it may be, and splendid though its achievements, was until the natural theologians came along intellectually on a level with the assertion in *Gulliver's Travels* that Mars had two moons – right, but undeservedly. It no more merits our respect than do the writings of Paul or John or other Christian theologians who sought to base their doctrines on revelation or experience.

Of course, all this leaves agnostics quite unmoved. It is only what they said all along, except that they are not convinced by the natural theologian either. Continuism suits their thought perfectly. Indeed, it strengthens their position very considerably in one respect at least. For notoriously some critics of Christianity, and of religion in general, have tried to explain religious experience away, and thereby to undermine at least one possible basis for belief. As we have seen, a continuist Christian has no real reply to them. Of course, individual attempts to explain religion away may prove unsuccessful; indeed, all attempts so far *have*. But if all religious experiences (including those of the supposed vehicles of revelation) are known in advance to be in principle explicable in natural terms without special divine action, which is what the continuist is obliged to admit, then these attempts are in a sense unnecessary; the point has already been conceded.

It is quite otherwise if discontinuity, and interaction between the divine and human levels is allowed. If it is, explaining religious experience away becomes immensely harder. For suppose that some fairly specious explanation of such experiences is advanced. Suppose it were shown (shall we say) that, whenever anyone went through an 'encounter with God', certain natural factors, perhaps a state of the brain, were present, and that whenever these factors were present, the experience always followed. Would this explain the 'encounter' away? Not in the least. Take an analogy. Certain states of the brain (and of the atmosphere) are doubtless present whenever I hear a piano sound middle C, and I have that experience whenever these states are present. But this does not show that there is no piano about the place. The natural factors present at the time of the experience may be necessary conditions for it to happen; but we cannot show that they are *sufficient* conditions for it unless we are able to show that they produce it when there is no piano – or no God – available to produce them.[7] In the case of the piano we can test this, by seeing if the same results are obtained with a recording of a piano, or an electronic device designed to simulate the sound of a piano. If they were, this would show that the experience was not *by itself* proof of the reality of the piano. But to achieve the corresponding result in the case of encountering God, we should have to show that God did not enter into the causal factors producing the experience. And since we cannot record God or simulate Him, this would have to be by showing (*a*) that there is no God; or (*b*) that He does not work in this sort of way – the continuist view; or (*c*) that He was not working in this way in this particular instance; or (*d*) that very similar natural factors normally lead to delusive 'experiences', so that there was a strong probability that the ones we were dealing with were delusory as well. Continuists have conceded (*b*) in advance; discontinuists have not. To meet them, therefore, the would-be refuter of religious experience has got to prove (*a*), (*c*) or (*d*) as well as producing the 'natural factors'. And that makes the task a great deal more difficult.

Notes

1. *The Remaking of Christian Doctrine* (London, SCM, 1974), p. 32
2. Ibid., p. 34
3. *Jesus Christ and Mythology* (London, SCM, 1960), pp. 60 ff.
4. Ibid., p. 62
5. Ibid., pp. 68-9
6. See my 'The Ethico-Theology of Immanuel Kant', *Journal of Theological Studies*, n.s., vol. 26 (1975), pp. 342 ff.
7. Strictly speaking, they could be sufficient conditions, provided that the piano was itself a necessary condition for *their* occurrence; but that is of course going to be no use to the continuist when applied in the case of God, and need not concern us here.

Interlude: The Analogy of Human and Divine

I have been arguing in the first part of this essay that God has created a world which is discontinuous as far as we human beings are concerned. It might be thought that a second part, arguing that it is also discontinuous as far as His own life and activity are concerned, would hardly be needed. 'What we will in our minds is translated into the movement of our limbs and our pens', writes Professor Bartholomew: 'it does not, therefore, seem too far-fetched to suppose that God is able to express his thoughts through matter in some analogous way.'[1] However, we do need to show that He does this. Professor Wiles, for one, is clear that He does not; it is his contention that human beings are free to choose and act in particular initiatives, but that God (doubtless by His own self-limitation) is not.[2] To this extent, therefore, Wiles cannot be called a strict continuist; he is only one where God is concerned.

He begins his defence of this rather surprising view by pointing out quite correctly that 'personal language in relation to God is a form of analogy...and not direct description. God is not a person as we are.' There are major differences between human personality and God's – e.g. human sexuality, or our need to acquire our knowledge gradually, through the senses. So far we may wholeheartedly agree. But if the power to *act* (except in the single initiatory act of creation) is missing, has not the analogy – which, as Wiles acknowledges, is the primary analogy for our speech about God – been evacuated of all real content? It seems queer to say that personality is the primary analogy for talk about God, and then to add that His (analogue to)

Interlude: The Analogy of Human and Divine 81

personality involves Him in no actions whatever except one – which is utterly unlike most of our actions in its nature.

There is a strong tradition that where language is used analogously about God it differs from the same language used about finite beings chiefly in that all *imperfections* in the finite analogue are conceived of as missing in the divine one.[3] Thus, to use Wiles' examples, sexuality, though not in itself a defect, is rooted in a severe limitation imposed on human life – the being confined, as far as this world is concerned, to mammalian bodies; while the gradual acquisition of knowledge through the senses is clearly a drawback from which God does not suffer. But the power to act on particular occasions is not a defect! The need to do so might possibly be regarded as one. If we thought it part of God's perfection that He should have planned everything in the world from first to last, with no idea of there being anything contrary to the plan (and thus, presumably, no room for human freedom), then special action would be a sign of imperfection; there would, after all, have been a flaw in the plan, which needed correcting. But neither Professor Wiles nor I think any such thing. Ability to act is not a defect, but a positive quality in a person, human or divine.

However, Wiles does not regard ability to act as a defect in itself; he thinks that God's non-intervention is a deliberate act of self-limitation. God's creation of the world necessarily involved a 'divine self-limitation in relation to traditional understandings of omnipotence and omniscience', so why not in this respect of non-intervention too?[4] The trouble is, the three are not really parallels. The first two do not involve a genuine self-limitation, only what one might call a logical one, which is really a limit, not on God or what he can do, but on what can intelligibly be said.

Consider omnipotence. If God creates partially independent beings with free wills of their own, is His omnipotence thereby limited? Not really. Wiles quotes with approval some words of Thomas Tracy,[5] that the creation of 'other agents', 'amounts to a purposeful limitation of the scope of his own activity, but it does not nullify his omnipotence'. That is correct.

God's power is no less; He has only chosen that in certain areas He will not normally exercise it. There is a self-limitation, but of scope, as Tracy says, not of onmipotence; the only sense in which the latter can be said to be limited is by the fact that God has created free agents and therefore cannot also make them unfree. In that sense omnipotence is 'limited' by the creation of a green leaf; for by creating it God has made it impossible for Himself to create a red leaf in the same time and place.

Consider omniscience, then. Wiles' only reason for speaking of a limitation here is the old fallacy that foreknowledge would entail a lack of freedom on the part of His creation, so that the creation's freedom entails lack of omniscience on the part of God. This is incorrect. God foresees a free act as free, and an unfree one as unfree; His knowledge does not affect them. Rather, it is the other way round; our actions affect what God knows (whether in advance or afterwards). 'The divine gaze looks down on all things without disturbing their nature.'[6] The only limitation is again a logical one: God cannot foresee an event *and* use that foreknowledge to prevent it, for if He did so it would not be there for Him to foresee. But this again is no real limitation: 'power to foresee the non-existent' is no real power, but a nonsensical collection of words.

The limitation which Wiles is proposing, however, is a real one: and it is far more extensive than the self-limitation involved in creating free agents. There, God simply declines to exercise His power over certain of the beings He creates – or, rather, decides to allow them a certain area of independence in which He will not as a rule intervene. In Wiles' picture of things, He is declining to act in any way anywhere in the whole of His created universe. And while the first is necessary in order to allow there to be freedom of will within the creation, what end is achieved by this second one?

Perhaps Wiles thinks this the only way in which God could make us truly free: He has to stand back completely once He has made the world. But this can hardly be right. Can we not appeal to our relationships with other people? My freedom is not destroyed by the fact that others have influenced my life. It may have been *limited* in certain ways (as it is by the laws that God has built into His creation). I was brought up by speakers of English, not of Urdu or Portuguese: and this has limited my freedom to converse with others. Even in moral and religious matters, we all know that people's beliefs and practices are affected by their upbringing and their contacts with others; and yet we acknowledge that they are reasonably 'free'. God might, then, allow Himself occasional contact with human beings and yet leave them the degree of freedom that (Wiles and I both agree) exists among us. And might it not be that that freedom, like other good human qualities and powers, is a pale reflection of that of the Lord? It is of course rash to say what the author of *Genesis* 1:26 had in mind when he pictured God as saying 'Let us make man in our image and likeness'. But certainly he goes on 'to rule the fish in the sea, the birds of heaven, the cattle, all wild animals on earth, and all reptiles that crawl upon it'. If men and women are to rule the world, and if they do so by acting on particular initiatives, and if God, in whose likeness they are made, also rules the world, it seems a reasonable conjecture that He too may act on particular initiatives.

I would add one other point. It is not only in regard to freedom that discontinuity occurs in human life – at least, not if the arguments I have been advancing are sound. In rationality and ethics, I have suggested, we meet with a different kind of discontinuity, in which, instead of our affecting the world (as in the exercise of freedom), or being affected by it (as in the case of our consciousness), we are affected by something 'outside' the world, by principles of logic or of goodness. That God wishes us to be reasonable and good is surely part of His purpose for us: the Lord bestows wisdom and teaches knowledge and understanding, and the righteous Lord loves righteousness. And it seems that in order to make this possible He has allowed the principles of understanding and righteousness to act on the world, making it differ from what it might otherwise have been. It seems strange that He should allow this, and yet restrain His own righteousness and wisdom from affecting us. In what follows, I hope to show that there are strong reasons for thinking that He has shown no such restraint – and for thanking Him for this.

Notes

1. *God and Chance*, p. 142
2. *God's Action in the World*, pp. 79-80
3. For an account of this, see e.g. Sherry, P.G., 'Analogy Today', *Philosophy*, vol. 51 (1976), pp. 431 ff.
4. Op. cit., p. 80
5. *God, Action and Embodiment* (Grand Rapids, Eerdmans, 1984), pp. 143-4, cited by Wiles, op. cit., p. 22
6. Boëthius, *Consolation of Philosophy*, V, vi Wiles actually refers to Boëthius, yet surely misses the point of what he is saying.

PART TWO

Providence and Miracle

The first part of this essay has, I hope, shown that no convincing account of human life can be given without admitting that in it the general continuity of nature is continually being interrupted. There would seem to be a good *prima facie* case, then, for supposing that any account of the Divine life (in so far as it is not an impertinence to talk of giving such an account) will also involve interruptions of that continuity. God made us in His image, we are told, and there may be a faint analogy between our life, with its little discontinuities, and His life, in so far as it relates to our universe, with its potentiality for far greater discontinuities. We do not, of course, know the Divine life from within as we do the human, so that the kind of arguments used in Part One will not as a rule be available to us; but we can look at what is usually believed by Christians to be the sort of thing God does, and see whether these look as if they involved discontinuity.

But first one possible misunderstanding ought perhaps to be cleared out of the way. I am not here considering what are usually called 'miracles', such as the healings worked by our Lord in the Gospels. I certainly believe that such miracles have taken place. But in a sense what I am trying to do is argue that there have been far *more* miracles than has usually been recognised; that the raising of Lazarus was only a more significant and more spectacular instance of a kind of Divine activity that is going on all the time. What marks out a 'miracle' as deserving special attention is partly the fact that it is obviously extraordinary, partly the fact that (in many cases at least) it has a special teaching function. The miracles of our Lord, it has been said, were 'acted parables' teaching the nature of God and His dealings with our race. Indeed, comparison of Mark 11:12-14,20 with Luke 13:6-9 suggests that Jesus could use both miracle and parable to make the same point. The Biblical miracles are therefore of great importance to the believer. But they do not (I shall be arguing) in principle differ from many less spectacular events, such as the promptings of God's grace, the insights of revelation, or the guidance of the Holy Spirit. All involve, or can involve, the kind of special action in the normal workings of the universe which we call 'miracle', even if they do not have the special meaning to be found in the Gospel miracles, nor take the form of stilling the waves, cleansing the leper, or raising the dead.

Such interaction, however, is by no means the only way God has of helping His creation, nor the normal one. The continuist is absolutely right to maintain that God normally helps us through His *general* providence. He has designed and created a universe in which there is room for life to appear and flourish, and for human life to seek after Him, and, it may be, find Him.[1] The laws and powers that prevail in the universe are His handiwork; it is thanks to them that we are able to exist; and when some good comes to us, and we thank God for it, it is almost invariably as a result of His general providence through these laws and powers.

It may be objected that while it is right and proper to thank God for these good things when they may be deemed part of His purpose, we often in practice thank Him on other occasions as well, and that this is not justified unless we believe in a special (miraculous?) intervention on His part. For example, the rising and setting of the sun make life much easier on earth. (Imagine a situation in which half the earth never knew a night and half never knew anything else!) We may well suppose that God intended this in His design of creation. But suppose that John proposes to Jane at a time when a particularly splendid sunset has put them both into a romantic mood; is it rational for them to thank God for the sunset as the origin of their later married happiness? It *may* be, of course, that from the beginning of creation He meant them to become engaged, in this way and at this particular time, and planned all things so as to bring this about: but it seems more likely that the beauty of that one individual sunset was simply an extra, a happy by-product of the divine purpose and providence.

All the same, I think that the gratitude of John and Jane is not altogether misplaced. This sort of gratitude is not unknown even where God is not involved. Suppose that in going to work I have to pass down a singularly dreary and dismal street, and that half-way along it someone has brightened it up with cheerful curtains and gay flowers in the window. One day I meet the housewife responsible. Is it not natural to say 'Oh, I must thank you for brightening up your window so! It cheers me up every time I pass it!'? And this though she certainly did not have any benefit to me in mind when she did it, and possibly no benefit to any passer-by at all. Much more, then, may Jane and John thank God, who, though doubtless He did not devise the sunset with their happiness as a part of His purpose, nevertheless foresaw that happiness and Himself rejoiced in it.

General providence, then, is the main source of God's care for His creatures. And it may be that from time to time He acts in a more special way with a miracle (whether recognised as such or not). But is there an intermediate kind of divine action as well, not strictly speaking an intervention in the world, and therefore not to be called miraculous, but nevertheless directed to a particular purpose rather than to the general well-being of the creation? This is what is known as an act of God's 'special providence'; a good definition has been given by M.J. Langford:[2] 'For the traditional account of providence to be maintained, it must be the case that God's action can make a difference to the world. At the same time, when we are speaking of providential action rather than of miracle, the action must be such that, after the event, a natural explanation is possible.' And if this can be done, such providential events will be quite compatible with continuism; and perhaps they will even enable us to do without miracle altogether.

Let us take a specific example to see what is being claimed

by those who believe in special providence. It will be recalled that when Paul and Silas were imprisoned at Philippi, there was an earthquake which led, indirectly, to the conversion of their gaoler (and to better conditions for the apostles).[3] Clearly we can suppose (in the absence of any explicit statement in the Bible) either that this was a miracle – there would have been no earthquake had not God deliberately sent one – or that it was just a coincidence, of great benefit (as it happened) to the gaoler and the apostles, but dependent on an earthquake that would have happened even had Paul and Silas never gone near Philippi. What we are being invited to consider as a third possibility is that the earthquake was indeed planned by God, but not as a miraculous intervention; rather, it took place by reason of the natural laws that govern earthquakes, only these were arranged so that it should have the effect that it did.

Now the natural way to understand this suggestion is to take it as holding that from the very moment of creation God was planning this incident, or, if there was no first moment of creation, that this was one of the fixed points that God had in mind in designing His eternal cosmos. So, of course, were all other cases of special providence. It is indeed possible to give a natural account of them after the event; but in actual fact all that preceded them, from creation or from eternity, was designed with these events in view.

We might compare an ingenious argument of Charles Babbage,[4] the father of computing, that all miracles might be the result of natural laws operating at a less perceptible level than they ordinarily do. The Calculating Engines he designed in the 1820s and 1830s could be so programmed (to use a modern expression) as to display numbers following a regular sequence, such as the consecutive numbers or their squares, but at some point to change the sequence to another, or even to display one number outside the sequence and then revert to the original pattern. The former would correspond to an alteration in the laws of nature, the latter to a miracle. But both would in fact be the expression of a perfectly law-abiding program on the Engine. And it is (Babbage believed) a higher proof of God's skill if He can do that sort of thing with nature than if He has to intervene to adjust the structure of His creation in order to accomplish His ends.

Although this idea of 'special providences' (not necesarily in Babbage's version!) may seem highly improbable, it is not logically impossible, given one very important condition. That is, that there is no free will; that every event, including every human act, is deliberately chosen by God. For otherwise the earthquake could, and indeed surely would, have failed of its purpose. Paul and Silas had to be brought to the gaol at Philippi on the crucial night; and it had to be that particular gaoler in charge, not one less easily disturbed by earthquakes, and so on. We may go further back, or rather, we *must* do so. For Paul, Silas and the gaoler to exist at all, it was necessary for their respective parents to marry one another, and no-one else and so on back through time. Even sins must be deliberately planned: for if the magistrates at Philippi had done their duty properly, Paul and Silas would not have been imprisoned at all. And so on...We have a full-blooded doctrine of Predestination on our hands, in its severest form, and with all its ethical and theological difficulties. Undoubtedly there have been many Christians who have felt able to accept such a doctrine, but not I think any of the modern continuists. It may be more skilful of God to produce His results by law, but it involves treating the personal part of His creation like – well, like components of a Calculating Engine.

It is, moreover, very hard to pick out what events *are* special providences: why pick out the earthquake rather than the marriage of Silas' maternal grandparents? Given any event which fulfils the divine purposes (such as the conversion of the gaoler), all events which lead up to it must be regarded as specially providential. And how do we know which events do fulfil the divine purposes, when our opinions on the subject may themselves lead to such an event, and may therefore have been planned in advance by God, whether they are true or mistaken? In attempting to defend the idea of special providences, we have not only had to concede universal predestination, we have found that that predestination swallows up the special providences themselves.

Another consideration which may be brought in here is this: if the indeterminism of present-day physics is soundly based (and unless we theologians are to lay down the law for scientists in advance, we must assume that it is), it is not possible for God to predestine the history of the universe, or of Earth, by laying down laws for it to follow, or rather, it is not possible that He has done so. (He might still predestine it by planning His own interventions ahead of time; but that breaks the continuity again.) For history depends on a vast number of undetermined events; there appears to be an enormous amount of sheer chance in it. And this is not just a matter of occasional sub-atomic events which have no real importance for us. It applies to the appearance of life, and to the mutations which allow life to develop and evolve. So much so that the molecular biologist Jacques Monod regarded this as clinching proof of the impossibility of there being purpose in the universe. This could be maintained for two reasons. Firstly, because there is no indication of a divine plan at the key points where mutations occur. They come about, to all appearances, in a completely haphazard sort of way. This point does not seem to me to be very strong. It would be perfectly possible for most mutations to be left to the general workings of the universe; if God directed only those which (let us say) led to the emergence of the human species, the impression given to the observer (not being privy to the thoughts of God) would still be one of haphazardness. (There would, after all, be nothing to distinguish the 'planned' mutations from any others, except that they did in fact lead to humankind and not to rabbits or cauliflowers as other mutations did.) Secondly – and here the Christian continuist ought to begin to feel embarrassed – because the element of chance means that without guidance the whole 'machine' rapidly gets out of control. If only a thousand mutations are required to produce intelligent life from a given starting-point, and if each of these could go in two ways, and only two, then when the series of mutations began the odds would have been 2^{1000} against the desired result's coming about. With such odds against Him, surely God would not have used such a method.

It is true, as Professor D.J. Bartholomew has pointed out,[5] that chance processes may lead to a predictable outcome. The result of a number of people's playing roulette will be a profit to the 'house' that can be calculated quite accurately; an infectious disease spread by homogeneous mixing of the population will eventually spread to everyone. So some aims can be achieved by means of random processes. The spread of the Gospel might be an instance: the spread, one might say, of an infectious health. More relevantly to our present concern, God might perhaps have planned that while life would only come into existence by chance, nevertheless it should be bound to come into existence *somewhere*. (There are in fact certain difficulties over accepting this, but we may let that pass.) There remains the awkward fact that nothing as specific as the appearance of the human race seems designable in this way. The owners of the gambling house can be sure of their profit, but not of which particular suckers will lose what particular sums; if I scatter breadcrumbs among birds in my garden, I may be sure that some will go to birds that are not starlings, but not that any will go to that particular finch. Dame Mary Warnock, I understand, has suggested as a possible answer (though not as her own belief) that the Creator might not have originally intended a result as specific as the human race, but could possibly have taken an interest in it once the human race did in fact result.[6] This is, curiously enough, the impression I have sometimes felt to be given by the creation narrative in *Genesis* 1, in which each stage of creation (each being declared 'good' in itself, by the way) is introduced by a decisive 'Let there be!', *except* for the creation of men and women, which seems almost to be an unplanned afterthought; it is not until plants and animals, fishes and birds are all established that the idea 'Let us make man in our own image, after our likeness' is mooted. But I doubt whether this was really what the author of Genesis had in mind.

The basic point is that if God had specific purposes of any kind in creating the universe, it was almost inevitable that He would have to act specially in order to ensure that the chance element in creation led it in the right direction. Either God controls all the apparent chance in the universe, or He controls some of it, or He creates all but controls none. The third, it would seem, makes any kind of purpose, except one in the form of a statistical probability (e.g. that there shall be a chance of 7.3% that a given galaxy shall contain life), virtually impossible. The second is discontinuist. There remains the first possibility – that all 'chance' is in reality directed by God. It looks like chance to us, because we cannot detect any sufficient cause for it (and indeed within the universe there is none to detect); yet in fact it is all the work of God. We are like the man in a satirical novel I once read, who studied the incidence of mute Es in French military writers of the twentieth century. If he discerned any pattern at all, it was purely statistical in nature – so many mute Es on average per page; but the writers he studied did not choose their words at random! Similarly, God's determination of events appears random to scientific investigation, because the factors that the scientist looks for are not the kind that figured in God's framing of His purpose. This seems to be the line taken by Dr E.L. Mascall in his Bampton Lectures: 'For the theist, nothing ever "just happens"... To the secondary cause it belongs merely to determine that there is a certain probability of the event occurring, and even this it does only as a result of its conservation by the primary cause which is God. To the primary cause alone it belongs to determine whether the event shall occur, and when and where; the secondary causes have no part or lot in this.'[7] Secondary causes – ordinary events in nature or history – give us a chance of $1/n$ that a given event (let us say a click on the loudspeaker attached to a Geiger counter, Dr Mascall's example) will take place. God decides whether and when the click will occur, though presumably His decisions are adjusted to ensure there is not much deviation from the $1/n$ ratio. Thus total predestination is retained; but it is at the cost of *constant* intervention by God. Every apparent undetermined event is in fact the result of a special decision by Him; He does not indeed break natural laws (He could, by ignoring the $1/n$

ratio), but He is constantly deciding what shall happen in individual events. Continuists cannot have their cake and eat it; perhaps they can do neither!

There remains, though, one very interesting possibility. I think it is what Langford had in mind in his book *Providence*, mentioned above; it is certainly advocated by Dr Polkinghorne in his *Science and Providence*.[8] And since Dr Polkinghorne is not only an extremely distinguished physicist but a Christian who is highly critical of what I have been calling 'continuism', he has to be listened to with respect. God's relationship to the world, he holds, 'must be characterised by the most profound consistency';[9] and therefore miracles must be 'perceptions of a deeper rationality...occasions which make visible a more profound level of divine activity'.[10] God's activity – His interaction with the world, to use the subtitle of Polkinghorne's book – will be personally consistent. But the world He has made is not a rigidly deterministic one, and there is room for divine interaction with what goes on in it, just as there is for human. Sub-atomic events, he holds (differing here from another physicist priest, Dr Pollard[11]), are unlikely to provide enough room for manœuvre. But is nature determinist even on a larger scale? 'The typical case [of dynamic behaviour] involves such an infinitesimally balanced sensitivity to circumstance (one might almost say, such a degree of vulnerability) that it results in an almost infinitely multiplying variety of possible behaviours...We are necessarily ignorant of how such systems will behave.'

This is the realm of what has become known as 'chaos theory', in which, 'given infinitesimally different starting points, systems can realise very different outcomes':[12] it has been summed up in such vivid pictures as the position of a billiard ball being affected by the gravitational attraction of a single electron at the edge of the galaxy or the flight of a butterfly in China affecting the weather in New York a week later. (Affecting on a large scale, that is! we are not talking of an occasional extra raindrop but of the difference between sun and storm.) But this is startlingly like the position where quantum events are concerned. There too we are necessarily ignorant of how events will go. And scientists have drawn the conclusion that the events themselves are undetermined. Why not with the larger scale events too? 'If you are a realist and believe, as I believe, that what we know (epistemology) and what is the case (ontology) are closely linked to each other,' says Dr Polkinghorne, 'it is natural to go on to interpret this state of affairs as reflecting an intrinsic openness in the behaviour of those systems.'[13] If so, of course, there is no problem over reconciling scientific determinism with interaction between God and His world; there *is* no scientific determinism – even where fairly large-scale events are concerned – to be reconciled. Sometimes, of course, we are dealing with systems which are simple enough for determinism to hold good: let us say, the movements of the solar system. Polkinghorne agrees with Wiles in his approval of Origen's remark that it would be absurd for someone suffering from midsummer heat to pray for the sun to be moved back into its springtime position.[14] But Wiles assumes that once this has been conceded we cannot really stop anywhere; Polkinghorne does not. The movements of the solar system are guaranteed by the divine reliability; but the detailed changes of the weather (within the general framework of the seasons) are so complex that whether God is or is not unvaryingly reliable to the extent that determinism supposes makes little difference. Meteorologists can predict these changes to some extent, but not completely – as we all know. God's 'immanent action' may therefore affect them *without* disturbing His reliability.

This may very well be right. My chief difficulty with it is the reason Polkinghorne adduces for believing in this wider indeterminism. With quantum events, there was reason *in principle* as to why we could never, even in theory, predict their future. With larger-scale events in complex systems, the impossibility is simply a result of the complexity; we are physically unable to work out the problem set us, but a Laplacean 'intelligence' would not be. It seems peculiar to reason (a) 'these systems are deterministic' (b) 'but thanks to their complexity and the "chaotic" nature of the equations that describe them it is not possible in practice to predict their future states' (c) 'since they are unpredictable we may assume that they are not deterministic after all'. Indeed, 'chaos effects' can be observed simply in the solution to mathematical equations: Dr Houghton suggests working out solutions to the formula $Y_{n+1} = aY_n - Y^2_n$ with minute variations in Y_0 and watching 'chaos' appear in the results. Yet it would be absurd to suggest that this equation had an 'intrinsic openness' which would enable God to affect its solutions. Moreover, the indeterminism of quantum events could be tested experimentally, and was, notably by Alaine Aspect: 'The Paris experiment,' writes Professor Davies, '...leaves little room for doubt that the uncertainty of the microworld is intrinsic. Events without causes, ghost images, reality triggered only by observation – all must apparently be accepted on the experimental evidence.'[15] What we know and what is the case are indeed related, but not in such a way as that what we cannot know cannot be; that would be nearer to idealism that to the realism Polkinghorne professes. Rather, what is the case affects what we can know. If complex systems are in principle unpredictable, they will also be so in practice, but not *vice versa*.

It may be, for all that, that they *are* unpredictable in principle as well as in practice. Popper has put this in the form of an epigram: classical physicists maintained (with a few exceptions) that clouds were really clocks (of immense complexity, naturally), but could equally well have held that clocks were really clouds (though far less in cloudiness than most other things).[16] There was no actual reason, even in classical physics, for believing in determinism; and since quantum physics has given strong reason for *dis*believing in it, we may as well scrap it altogether. It applies only to very severely constrained systems (like clocks, or the solar system); it does not apply to large systems like a cloud of gnats or the sun, nor for that matter to a soap-bubble. In a clock, 'the controlling mechanisms are designed to suppress, or compensate for, all cloud-like effects as far as possible'; in the bubble, a cloud-like system (the air enclosed in the bubble) is 'plastically and softly controlled' by another cloud-like system, the soapy film.[17] So it may be that we do not need to suppose that God's interaction with the world is always in the form of 'miracle', that is, doing something which but for His action would have been determined along different lines by other elements in the world; perhaps He is simply interacting with undetermined elements in it – that is, ones He Himself has left undetermined by other elements. But this is small comfort to the continuist. For it does not eliminate discontinuity; it extends it. The very fabric of nature is uncertain and plastic, whether to alteration by human action or by God's.

THE PROBLEM OF EVIL

The existence of evil is notoriously a difficult problem for theism; its opponents would sometimes claim that it is an insuperable one. But it looks as if the problem were made more acute still if we take the 'discontinuist' line I have been defending. Not, indeed, where the solution to part of the problem is seen in the fact of human freedom. Here discontinuity makes things easier, not harder; the fact that we are free to do good or evil means that the responsibility for the good or evil that we choose to do is ours and not God's. He gave us the power to choose, and is therefore responsible for the *possibility* of moral evil; but for its *actuality* we must bear the blame. Such a defence is not open to the continuist; not, that is, to a wholly consistent one. Some, as we have seen, accept human freedom but not God's.

It is another matter when we consider God's activity in His universe and the existence of 'physical' evil. If the continuist is correct, God has designed His universe to function according to certain laws, and does not now intervene to disturb their functioning. These laws cannot always suit the wishes of us humans (or other sentient beings), for they have to be framed in terms which do not refer to wishes at all. They do in fact work for our good on the whole, but every now and then they are bound to work against us. The existence of gravity keeps us from flying off into space as the earth spins, but it also injures us, and can even kill us, when we fall from a height. Nevertheless, the laws on the whole are tolerable enough, far more tolerable than chaos would be. That there should *be* laws is plainly good, and God may therefore be felt to have done well in creating this world, despite the evils that occur in it, for, given the existence of sentient beings in a law-governed universe, some evils are bound to occur.

But does this hold good if we take the discontinuist line? The point was made forcefully, perhaps too much so, by Bishop David Jenkins in a speech to the General Synod of the Church of England on 6 July 1986.

> We are faced, [he said] with the claim that God is prepared to work knock-down miracles in order to let a select number of people into the secret of his incarnation, resurrection and salvation, but he is not prepared to use such methods in order to deliver from Auschwitz, prevent Hiroshima, overcome famine or bring about a bloodless transformation of apartheid... If such a God... actually exists, then he must be the very devil.[18]

If we can push past such rather unworthy language as 'very devil' or 'knock-down miracles' (or, elsewhere, 'divine laser-beams'), we find quite a serious point. If God never acts in His universe, then clearly He does not act to prevent Auschwitz or Hiroshima. But if He does act in it, and more especially (though this was not the Bishop's argument) if He does so quite often, as I am suggesting and as Christianity has traditionally held, surely Auschwitz and Hiroshima, famine and apartheid are obvious occasions for Him to have done so. Yet He did not. Therefore, if He exists at all, He does not do what he ought, and is not the *good* God Christians believe in. And conversely, if He *is* the good God Christians believe in, and yet did not intervene in these cases, He clearly does not intervene at all.

This looks a strong case; but it is not in fact nearly as strong as it looks. One preliminary point ought certainly to be made. Discussions of the 'problem of evil' have almost always included somewhere what is usually known as the 'Free Will Defence'. God, it is argued, has made men and women free agents, able to do good and evil, free even to sin if so they choose. That is necessary if there is to be genuine moral good in the world. But if He has made us free, clearly He can hardly be intervening all the time to take away that freedom by preventing its misuse or frustrating it when it *is* misused.[19] And the instances cited by Dr Jenkins were all instances where human choice and activity were at work. (Famine is no exception. The famines of the world today could be dealt with if the will were there; but governments prefer spending money on armaments for killing people to spending it on food to save them, and the public – or so they assume, though I have my doubts – prefer low prices and tax-rates to helping those whom higher ones would benefit.) As far, then, as Dr Jenkins' examples are concerned, continuists are actually in a weaker position than their opponents.

However, this is only a preliminary point. Other evils besides those four do exist. (It is possible, indeed, that some *past* famines were not avoidable by human action.) More crucial is the reply that, despite apearances, continuists are no better equipped to explain the troubles of the world than we others are; possibly less so. Consider the continuists' argument again. God does (it is alleged by their opponents) act on the world from time to time, e.g. in the Incarnation and Resurrection. Surely He has at least as good reason to intervene to prevent natural disasters, even if not man-made ones, as He had for these other special actions? As He does not act to stop the disasters, either He is not the God of love both sides believe Him to be, or else He does not intervene elsewhere either.

But this argument can be turned back against its users. God (they allege) does not intervene in the world, though He could, for He is omnipotent. 'It is no part of my argument, exploration and meditation to say...that God cannot do that' (*viz.* work on physical matter to bring about saving miracles), declares Dr Jenkins;[20] and a special relationship of God to a particular event, says Wiles, 'is not to be excluded in advance as logically impossible'.[21] Why, then, has He not chosen to break His general rule and intervene to stop these natural disasters? Any reason that continuists can adduce can also be adduced by discontinuists (with one exception which we shall come to later). For example, does God wish the world to be governed by law in such a way that science, or indeed a reasonable life, is possible? The discontinuists agree; only they think that this governance need not be, and is not, absolutely invariable. Either the special actions we are imagining, to prevent great disasters, would have to be so great as to injure people by disrupting the general rule of law, or they would not. In the first case God has sufficient reason not to break His general practice (according to continuists, His invariable practice); neither side need worry. In the second case He apparently ought to make this one of His instances of special action (according to discontinuists) or He ought to break His otherwise invariable practice (according to continuists); both sides are equally embarrassed. Perhaps the discontinuists are the better off really. For all they know, God may have acted on lots of occasions to prevent natural disasters when this could be done with safety; it is simply that we do not know of them. (*Amos* 7:1-6 is perhaps relevant here?) This is not a possibility for their opponents; for them, God has never acted to prevent *any* disaster, and never will.

One reason that continuists might adduce (though I should be surprised if they did) which is barred to their opponents is this: Perhaps God sets so high a value on regularity in the universe (considered purely for its own sake, and not for any effects it has on us) that *nothing* will induce him to disturb it. But this is of course intolerable. Firstly, all the argument of chapters 1-5 above has gone, I hope, to show that He does *not* value regularity all that highly; that, on the contrary, He has built all kinds of irregularities into His world. Secondly, because this is not the 'loving, identifying and gracious God' to whom Dr Jenkins rightly referred elsewhere in his speech. It is a clockmaker who seems to be so in love with the workings of his machinery that he subordinates all other needs and purposes to it. If we really have to use language like 'he must be the very devil', this seems the place to use it. At least the purposes which the Bishop thought so inadequate to provoke divine action were better than this: the salvation of the human race, the defeat of sin and death, and the breaking down of the barriers between God and His people are nobler ends than the preservation of mechanical regularity in the universe.

An alternative – again one which I do not think many continuists would wish to use – would be to say, not that God will not act on His world, but that He *cannot* do so. Perhaps at the creation He bound Himself to refrain from all such action; and even He cannot break that bondage. This would mean abandoning both omnipotence (as it is logically impossible for an almighty God to bind Himself irrevocably) and omniscience (as presumably He cannot have realised the consequences of His decision, or we should be back with a renewed 'problem of evil'). This seems a high cost to pay.

The problem of evil, and why God allows it, is a serious one indeed, and no Christian theologian can afford to take it lightly. But we do not solve it by eliminating God from the workings of the world. As a matter of fact, to recall a point made in chapter 5 (and to anticipate the discussion in chapter 12), we probably make it more acute. For if God does not act upon the world, He does not reveal Himself through actions, only through the general structure of the world as a whole. And in that case our belief in a God of love, compassion and grace must be inferred from that structure – which is not easy to do. In the heyday of natural theology, the goodness of God was commonly deduced *a priori*;[22] but not many would wish to attempt this today. And to deduce it *a posteriori* from nature – well, David Hume summed it all up admirably. 'There is no view of human life or of the condition of mankind from which, without the greatest violence, we can infer the moral attributes or learn that infinite benevolence, conjoined with infinite power and infinite wisdom, which we must discover by the eyes of faith alone.'[23] I should say, by the light of revelation alone: Hume, for his sceptical purposes, has put his point in such a way as to make the believer's position look as unreasonable as he can. But as far as the continuist believer is concerned, he is surely right; for the continuist's faith, unless it is indeed based on the *a priori*, can be based on nothing at all – neither revelation nor observation. And thus the problem of evil becomes a problem, not of how we can reconcile our belief in God's love with the reality of evil, but why we should believe in a God of love at all in the first place.

Notes

1. Acts 17:27. It is of interest that some contemporary scientists, by no means sympathetic to Christianity or other religions, have seen in the signs of a general providence aiming for life the best evidence for the reality of a God, perhaps a finite one. Cf. e.g. Davies, P., *God and the New Physics* (pbk edn, Harmondsworth, Penguin, 1984), pp. 187-9; Hoyle, F., *The Intelligent Universe* (London, Joseph, 1983), pp. 218-9

2. *Providence* (London, SCM, 1981), p. 87

3. Acts 16:25 ff.

4. *Ninth Bridgewater Treatise* (London, Murray, 1837), chaps 2 and 8

5. *God of Chance* (London, SCM, 1984), pp. 73 ff.

6. Cited by Bartholomew, op. cit., p. 8, from Lewis, J. (ed.), *Beyond Chance and Necessity* (Garnstone, 1974), p. 12

7. *Christian Theology and Natural Science* (London, Longmans, 1956), p. 201

8. London, SPCK, 1989

9. Op. cit., p. 6

10. Op. cit., p. 51, cf. also 'A Note on Chaotic Dynamics', *Science and Christian Belief*, I, 2 (1989), pp. 123 ff.

11. *Chance and Providence* (London, Faber, 1958)

12. Houghton, J.T., 'New Ideas of Chaos in Physics', *Science and Christian Belief*, I, 1 (1989), p. 42

13. Polkinghorne, op. cit., pp. 28-9

14. Origen, *On Prayer*, 5, 3, cited by Polkinghorne, op. cit., p. 31, and Wiles, *God's Action in the World*, p. 100

15. *God and the New Physics*, pp. 106-7

16. Abridged from his Compton Memorial Lecture, 'Of Clouds and Clocks', in *Objective Knowledge* (2nd edn, Oxford, 1981), pp. 210-13

17. Popper, op. cit., pp. 249-50

18. *God, Miracle and the Church of England* (London, SCM, 1987), p. 5

19. I do not forget divine grace; but I believe this to operate on free human wills.

20. Op. cit., p. 4

21. *The Remaking of Christian Doctrine*, p. 36

22. E.g. St Thomas Aquinas' *Summa contra Gentiles*, I, 28, 37, 75 and 91

23. *Dialogues concerning Natural Religion*, part X

History

Christianity, it has frequently been said, is an historical religion, and this in two senses. Firstly, certain events in past history are crucially important to it, in a way that does not apply to most other religions. Of course, many other religions (Hinduism and Shinto being exceptions) have had founders or other great teachers who have lived in times past and whose importance to the religion is obvious. But in most cases they are important because of the content of what they taught, not because of their lives in themselves (except as examples). The Buddha is only the most recent of many Buddhas who reached the same enlightenment; Muhammad is the seal of a line of prophets all commissioned to proclaim the same basic message. But in Judaism and Christianity certain events – the election of Israel for both, the life, death and resurrection of Jesus for the latter – are important in themselves. There is teaching not only in them but through them.

Secondly, Christianity (in common with Judaism, Islam and Zoroastrianism) has a particular view of the sweep of history which is not shared by other religions, nor by secular thought. The historical process is not (it is claimed) haphazard, neither is it circular (as in Hindu or Stoic thought); it is linear, with a definite and very important goal set for it by God. 'Christians,' writes Dr David Bebbington, 'have normally adhered to these three convictions about history: that God intervenes in it, that he guides it in a straight line; and that he will bring it to the conclusion that he has planned.'[1] Our present question will therefore be whether we can retain the last two of these (modified if necessary) without the first, which is clearly incompatible with continuism; and similarly whether we can retain belief in the religious significance of certain historical events without this idea of divine intervention.

I confess that there is one of Dr Bebbington's 'convictions' about which I feel some hesitation. Can we really say that God guides history in *a straight line*? If this is meant to deny that He guides it in a *circle*, and no more, it is correct. But if it means that every point along the line is laid down, and nearer to the goal than any that preceded, this seems to me both unbiblical and intrinsically unlikely. There are many passages in the Bible where it seems clear that more than one possibility was open; where, so to speak, two or more possible histories diverge, and where it is mortals, not God, who choose between them. The Fall is an obvious example; but there are many others (e.g. Deuteronomy 28 or Jeremiah 38:17). No doubt there were certain fixed points which were certain to be led up to by one route or another (cf. Esther 4:14), but this does not mean that the path itself was irrevocably fixed. What is more, thanks to human folly and sin, the line of history at times diverges from what God seems to have wanted. It is not a straight line; it wobbles.

Now God's guidance of history has normally been seen in terms of divine interventions. He intervened to call Abraham, to deliver the Israelites from slavery, to give them the Law, to call first Saul and then David to the throne, and of course above all to come in the person of His Son to redeem mankind: He has doubtless been at work on His Church ever since as well, even if there is some disagreement about exactly where: and He will intervene decisively at the final Day of the Lord, to 'bring it to the conclusion that he has planned'. How, it may be wondered, can even a shadow of all this be retained if the idea of special divine actions is abandoned?

One possible answer would be, yet again, total predestination. We can avoid the idea of God's acting in particular events, and yet picture Him as guiding history, by supposing that He planned every event in His act of creation, leading up no doubt to a demythologised Last Day. The 'wobbles' of which we spoke just now would not, then, arise from there really being more than one possibility open to people; they would probably arise from the fact that God only operates by laws, so as to avoid special actions, and cannot do this while at the same time effecting an orderly and direct progress towards His final goal. King Zedekiah's failure to heed the advice of Jeremiah was not itself specifically intended by God for its own sake; He would in fact, we may well suppose, have preferred (other things being equal) that Zedekiah should listen; but his refusal was caused by pre-existing factors (physical, psychological, or whatever) which could not be avoided, nor prevented from leading to the refusal, except by divine intervention. There had therefore to be a deviation from the straightest line of divine purpose – the deviation which we know as the Babylonian Captivity. God is thus the author, albeit one hopes the reluctant author, of all human sins, crimes and follies; and although this position has been defended, I do not myself think it true, biblical or Christian.

However, perhaps we can avoid this, and leave some room for human freedom, by supposing that God operates by *laws of history*, superimposed on the laws of science. On this view, God has built into His world, or rather into that part of it which consists of human lives and communities, laws which ensure that if (for example) the advice of His prophets is heeded by kings and rulers, they and their peoples will avoid exiles which otherwise they would have undergone. These laws produce results which make it look as if God were reacting to individual events, but in fact no divine intervention is required. We might compare the programming of a computer to play chess. It looks as if it were handling each move by its opponent freely on its individual merits; actually, it operates according to the laws of its program, and there is nothing about it to disturb the most sensitive continuist. And the laws of history are designed to further God's purposes in the same sort of way as the computer's program is designed to make it win the game.

This looks a lot more promising. It avoids, for once, total predestination; for human acts, or some of them, may be perfectly free (just as the computer does not control its opponent's moves), yet it also avoids special divine actions in the world. Yet it has its own difficulties. In the first place, it is not what the Bible depicts as the way God deals with history. And this is important, whatever our views on Biblical authority and inspiration, because the Bible is the only real source for our belief that God has any plan at all for the human race; it is the reason for our having an 'historical religion'. However, this is not a fatal objection. We might easily describe our chess-playing computer as avoiding a trap set by its opponent, or deciding to sacrifice its Queen, or preparing to castle, even though in each case the move was really implicit in its program. And similarly it could be that God was described in the Bible as choosing Israel, or sending prophets, even though He did so solely by means of the laws He had built into human history. It is just that the language in which His dealings with us are described has been simplified.

More serious is the charge that it is not the Biblical picture of God's *character*. He is supposed to be just, for example, and merciful, and loving. But surely these are qualities which can only be exhibited in personal relationships, not in a 'programming' of history before history began? Justice we *might* be able to understand in an impersonal way; judges, after all, are expected not to be personally involved with those whose cases they try. Mercy would be harder, but even that might be depersonalised, becoming closer to *leniency*. But is it even conceivable that *love* should be fitted into this theory's mould? The most you could say would be that God had designed the laws of history in such a way that in certain circumstances they would produce the sort of result that would also have been produced if He had acted in the world out of love for it, or for Israel, or for the Church, or for an individual man or woman. But we should not have the slightest reason to suppose that He actually did love anybody; it is all a completely impersonal affair from start to finish.

And of course there is the additional difficulty that it is not at all clear what these laws of history might be. Some in times past have evidently supposed they were fairly simple ones like 'The good shall prosper and the evil shall not'; but the book of Job is explicit that this is not so – as much of ordinary human experience proves. Certainly people have attempted, and even at times claimed, to discover more subtle laws than this in history: the names of Hegel, Marx and Toynbee occur to one. But none of the laws that they claimed to have discovered has met with universal agreement.

Now undoubtedly laws may and do exist without being detected. This applied to the greater part of physical science for thousands of years; might it not also be true of history? Yes, it might, but there were good reasons for thinking scientific laws were there to be discovered; elementary ones like the alternation of day and night or summer and winter were known about as soon as *anything* was known. Are there good reasons for thinking the same applies to history? The principle of continuism by itself will not do. If scientific laws exist and apply universally, then continuity is assured whether or not there are laws in any disciplines other than those of the natural sciences. There are no *a priori* reasons for believing in laws of history.

This is not absolutely decisive. It would still be open to someone to argue 'I believe' (for some reason) 'that God has purposes in history. I am sure He cannot, or will not, seek to achieve them by taking an active part in history Himself; I cannot see that scientific laws by themselves will achieve His ends; I must therefore believe that He has designed history to operate by laws of its own which further His purposes, even though I am not at present in a position to say what those laws are.' Similarly 'I am sure that this computer is intended to win this game; I am also sure that it is not alive and purposefully planning its moves; I must therefore believe that it is programmed to make its moves according to an intelligently devised scheme, even though I do not yet know what the program is.' But at least with the computer one can see that it is 'trying' to win, and one can make a guess, from one's own knowledge of the game, what *sort* of rules are likely to be embodied in its program. It does not appear that we can do either where God's governance of history is concerned

– at least, not without an appeal to the Bible or some other source of revelation, which seems to let special action in (both because the Bible depicts God as intervening in the world, and because revealing is itself, as we shall see, a form of special action).

An alternative way of trying to reconcile continuism with divine governance of history would be some kind of 'demythologising' of the latter. The picture the Bible gives us of God's purposive dealings with peoples and communities is to be understood as no more than a picture; the reality is that He has purposes for individuals, and only for them. This is most plausible when we are dealing with the *culmination* of God's purposes. Most would agree that peoples and communities – even Israel and the Church militant – will cease after the final consummation, whereas individuals will not. Might it not be that the Biblical picture of Judgment Day and the final victory over evil is to be seen, not as the end of *all* history, so much as the end of *each* (personal) history? Each and every individual will eventually be judged, and God's triumph over evil will be seen in that person (whether by punishment or by redemption). In the process, of course, all mankind will be judged; but it is the individual 'history' that matters, not the collective, and the divine judgment, being outside this universe of space and time, does not affect its continuity.

Now there is certainly a good deal to be said for this. Many descriptions of the Last Things in the Bible are clearly couched in the language of symbolism; and it has always been something of a problem in Christian eschatology why there should need to be two Judgments, one at death and one at the General Resurrection. Maybe the latter *is* in reality only a picture of the former. And if the only dealings God were supposed to have with history were those at its end, we might concede the continuist's case. But they are not. The normal idea is that the Last Things are only the climax to a relationship which has been going on since first our race appeared. And while the traditional picture of Judgment Day might be seen as a statement in 'mythical' form of the ultimate sovereignty of the Lord and the need for each of us to face His justice as well as His mercy, it is not easy to see how the rest of God's alleged dealings with us in history could be interpreted in this way. The authors of such works as *The Myth of God Incarnate*[2] would presumably so interpret the Incarnation and the Atonement, but, even apart from the deficiencies of such works, the Incarnation and Atonement are not the only preeschatological deeds ascribed to God. (Jews and Muslims, of course, believe that God has acted in history, but *not* in an Incarnation or an Atonement!) To give a 'mythical' interpretation to the Exodus, the covenant with David, the sending of the prophets, or the Exile and Return is surely impossible, without reverting to the unnatural allegorising methods of some Alexandrian Fathers. We may claim that God was not at work in any of these events (except in the sense that He is at work even in the fall of a sparrow), or we may claim that He was, or we may suspend judgment. We cannot treat them as mythological portrayals of eternal truths. And if we cannot treat them as examples of God's general purpose either, I think that continuists have got to reject the idea that Christianity is in any sense an historical religion. They are of course at liberty to do so. But I must admit that to me at any rate there seems little point in calling the result 'Christian'.

THE INCARNATION

It might seem at first that the Incarnation was *the* supreme instance of an intervention (or alleged intervention) by God in human history and indeed I believe precisely that. But it is worth seeing what sort of an account of the Incarnation might theoretically be given by a continuist. In trying to do so I was surprised to find how much of the orthodox teaching could be retained. There are of course continuists who deny the Incarnation, except perhaps as an allegory or 'myth', but I am not concerned with such here. I want to imagine a continuist who sincerely wishes to retain a full belief in Jesus Christ as the Word of God made flesh and dwelling among us. Such people may not exist, except as figments of my imagination, but I think they would be able to say a surprising amount for themselves, even if in the end it turned out to be not quite enough.

In the first place, they could point out that all Jesus' words and deeds were unquestionably the words and deeds of a complete and genuine human being. He was born, grew up, and died; He walked, spoke, slept, ate and drank. Even His miracles were performed with human words and gestures, and had precedents and successors among the prophets and the apostles; even His Resurrection was that of a human body. To say that any of His actions were *not* human would certainly be close to heresy in traditional terms (if indeed 'close' is not an understatement). It has usually been supposed that what did set Jesus apart from others was, firstly, that in Him God was uniquely at work, and secondly, that through Him God was bearing the sins of His people. Now it is the latter that appears most of all to require a full Incarnation. Without it, we should only have a good man suffering horrible injustice, which could never redeem the world; with it, it is God Himself who suffers with and among us, bearing His own wrath. But this requires no discontinuity in history, indeed, no *act* of God upon history. God and man are one in Jesus Christ, says the 'Athanasian Creed', 'not by conversion of the Godhead into flesh, but by taking of the manhood into God'. The manhood is part of this world, but is assumed by God the Son, so that what is done to Jesus of Nazareth is in fact, whether the world realises it or not, done to God. But all this calls for no action of God upon the world; it is, if anything, the other way round, the world acting, terribly, upon God. The discontinuity is in heaven, not on earth; we can, therefore, be continuists and yet still retain a full-blooded doctrine of the Incarnation (and indeed of the Atonement).

And as far as the heart of incarnational Christology is concerned I am bound to admit that this is true. I am not sure that anyone has ever held it, but if they have I cannot quarrel with them. Yet the heart is not the whole. In Jesus God is not only passive but active as well: He is not only the Sacrifice but also the Revealer. Indeed, modern Christologies have tended, if anything, to make this aspect of His life and work more important than the other. I believe this is an error; but that this aspect does exist is surely undeniable. And in that case we are back to discontinuity again, especially when we remember Christ's own emphasis on the supremacy of the Father's will in His life: 'The Son can do nothing by himself; he does only what he sees the Father doing; what the Father does, the Son does.'[3] Indeed, this applies not only to Christ's revealing work but to His saving work also; here too He came to do the work of the One who sent Him. There is a direct causal link between the Father's plan and the Son's execution of it.

As a matter of fact, even if this were not so, there would still be something a little disquieting to continuism in the Incarnation. For, as we saw just now, even if we supposed for the sake of argument that no breach of continuity was required on earth to let the Son be incarnate, still there was discontinuity required in heaven; very great discontinuity. God has taken to Himself the humanity of Jesus of Nazareth, a thing which is hardly a necessity of the divine nature! God might have never been incarnate, and yet still have been God; millions, of course, believe precisely that. If God, however, behaves, or lives, in so discontinuous a manner, does it not suggest that He may have let this discontinuity, or others, affect His world also?

With the Incarnation are linked, traditionally, several other apparent special actions of God – the Virgin Birth, the Atonement, the Resurrection, and the Ascension. Of these, the Resurrection is the one which most concerns us. For the Virgin Birth, which if it took place would certainly have needed divine intervention, has by many been felt not to be absolutely vital to Christian belief. I am inclined to think myself that it is in reality closely bound up with the idea of Incarnation, but to argue this would take us too far from our main subject. So let it be assumed for the sake of the discussion that the Virgin Birth can be set on one side.

The Atonement is the heart of the Gospel and it is certainly true that some continuists have sought to detach it from any connection with Jesus of Nazareth (except the historical one, so that the events which lead to our 'atonement' with God can be traced back to him). This is not perhaps necessary. Though the Atonement involves a mighty change in the way things are, it is, once again, in large part a change on God's side. I do not mean to take the crude line which says that until Calvary God was angry with us, but that the crucifixion of His Son soothed Him: the whole process of the Atonement springs from a divine love which was there all along. The change is that God has done something He need not have done, and that as a result a salvation is open to us that need not have been. In so far as it is a change in God, it does not involve discontinuity here in earth. And in so far as it is a change in us, reconciling us to God, this is done (it could be urged) through the historical events which link us and our reconciliation to Christ and His Cross.

The Ascension could probably be interpreted in continuist terms – given the Resurrection – by seeing it *negatively*, as the last of the Lord's appearances in physical form to His disciples. But this depends on a belief in the Resurrection itself; and it is to this that we must turn. As traditionally understood, this is one of the greatest discontinuities in history; in its effects and in its significance, perhaps the greatest of all. And even if it is not understood in the traditional way we are little better off. Even if we ignore the accounts of the empty tomb – and the reasons adduced for doing so seem to me exceedingly flimsy – how do we square the accounts of the resurrection-appearances with a 'closed weft of history'[4] view? Dead men do not normally appear, even in visions, to their friends, nor expound the Scriptures to them; ghosts are, surely, just as objectionable to the continuist as resurrections. Of course, *hallucinations* are acceptable, we know that they happen in nature; but to call the resurrection-appearances 'hallucinations' is to imply that Jesus was *not* risen, even in the weakest of senses, or at least that we have not the slightest reason to think that He was. Maybe this is what Wiles is maintaining in his brief discussion in *God's Action in the World*,[5] although what he says is rather sketchy, perhaps only tentative, and certainly not easy to follow. 'Historical reflection', he writes, 'by itself cannot determine the nature of such appearances and visions.' This we may agree with (in the suspension of any belief in the empty tomb). And faith in Jesus' vindication , and life with God, need not have derived from supernatural appearances. Presumably, then, he regards the appearances as not supernaturally but naturally given and, if the accounts of the empty tomb are rejected, it seems to follow that the appearances were natural in the same way that other hallucinations are. On the other hand, since Wiles seems uncertain about whether the empty tomb traditions *are* to be rejected, it may be that I have misunderstood him.

There are some scholars, such as Schillebeeckx,[6] who seem to discard both the 'empty tomb' narratives *and* the 'appearance' ones as later developments. What was crucial was not a vision or a discovery that the body of Jesus had disappeared, but a kind of 'conversion experience' which was 'presented in the form of an appearance vision'. But of course this makes no real difference. Was the 'conversion' simply a matter of human psychology, or was it an act of grace on God's part? If the former, it is no basis for any sort of Christian assertion. The workings of a few first-century Jewish minds have in themselves no theological significance. However, Schillebeeckx himself seems to favour the latter: 'what is called the "appearing", then, is obviously not to be characterised as an occurrence deriving merely from human psychology; on the contrary, it is described as an initiative of Jesus himself, as a gracious act of Jesus Christ: God in Christ is party to it.'[7] In that case, once again, we have a special act of God breaking the continuity. It is not, admittedly, an act described in any of the narratives, except as a *result* of the appearances or the discovery of the empty tomb, but it is still an act of God.

Willi Marxsen is still more extreme in his attitude to the New Testament narratives, and half inclined to replace 'Jesus is risen' by 'Jesus comes today' or the like; yet he insists on describing this version of Resurrection as a miracle, and is quite explicit that 'theologically speaking, one can only talk of a miracle if one is claiming divine intervention'.[8] Even here the Christian content of the Resurrection, however attenuated that content may seem to the traditionally orthodox, has to be seen as something in which God Himself is directly at work. If Jesus comes today, this breaks the continuity: unless one merely means that there are still effects today arising from what happened in his lifetime, which is clearly *not* what Marxsen wants to say, and would be equally true of Pontius Pilate.

Continuists, therefore, must not merely reject the traditional idea of a bodily Resurrection, they must also deny that Jesus is risen in any sense which is not equally true of – well, let us leave Pilate out of it and say St Polycarp. No doubt Jesus' faith in God[9] was justified, and He lives now with the Father in glory, but the same could be said of Polycarp. I say 'no doubt', but of course there is no reason why the continuist should believe in either. Any *evidence* that Jesus was vindicated or glorified would have to come from the heaven in which this was effected, and would therefore be an unacceptable intrusion into the continuity of the world. Certainly a 'leap of faith' is required of any believer. We cannot *prove* that Jesus rose again, and if we could, it would not *prove* His Sonship. But it would certainly be relevant evidence. The conservative believer, who accepts the New Testament picture of what happened at the first Easter, and the liberal believer, who accepts the appearances as veridical, both have some relevant evidence for their faith, something that makes it look fairly rational, even though far from proven. Even the thorough-going radical, who thinks only in terms of *present-day* faith, thinks of that faith as a gift from a God, a response to a Christ, who is active at the present day. It may be difficult to give a reasonable ground for that faith, but if the faith is justified at all it is God's direct work. However continuist believers have to believe even though they *reject* as worthless all the evidence associated with the Resurrection, regarding their own faith as something produced by purely natural means, like the belief of others in astrology. Or, of course, they may disbelieve: hold that Jesus no longer exists, or at least cannot be known, nor reasonably be supposed, to exist any longer. Atheists will, naturally, be happy to accept this; but few will feel it is quite so readily compatible with Christianity.[10]

Notes

1. Bebbington, D., *Patterns in History* (Leicester, IVP, 1979), p. 43
2. Ed. Hick, J., (London, SCM, 1977)
3. John 5:19.
4. Bultmann's phrase; see Bartsch, H. (ed.), *Kerygma and Myth*, i (London, SPCK, 1953), p. 197
5. Pp. 92-3
6. Cf. *Jesus* (ET London, Collins, 1979), pp. 329 ff.
7. Op. cit., p. 347 Schillebeeckx, like some other radical theologians, is an annoyingly elusive writer. It is seldom clear whether he is reporting his own views or those of others which he does not himself share. In this passage, for instance, the words 'obviously not to be characterised' suggest that we today are not to think of what happened as deriving merely from psychology, but the words 'described as an initiative' suggest that he is thinking simply of what Paul is trying to say (I Cor. 15:3-8 is being discussed). Similarly, on p. 390 we find him using the words 'the reporting of what happened in the guise of appearances': was what *occurred* in the guise of appearances, or was it only the reporting? A footnote (n. 119 on p. 710) repudiates any kind of 'rationalism'. 'There are always inter- mediary historical factors in occurrences of divine grace. The appearances form no exception.' But having apparently committed himself to one side of the fence, Schillebeeckx promptly covers himself – or spoils the effect – by adding 'Faith is emasculated if we insist on grounding it in pseudo-empiricism, thereby raising all sorts of false problems: whether, for instance, this Christological mode of seeing was... "objective" or "subjective" seeing.' But in so far as one can make out what Schillebeeckx's own views are, they seem to be incompatible with continuism.
8. *The Resurrection of Jesus of Nazareth* (ET London, SCM, 1970), p. 140
9. If we can use this expression; the Bible does not. Jesus is often presented as the object of faith; never, I think, as its subject.
10. See also chapter 11, 'Revelation' pp. 141-2, below.

Prayer

Even the most cursory glance at any collection of Christian prayers or liturgies will yield a large number of requests to the Deity to intervene in the world, or thanks to Him for having done so. (And indeed the same holds for many non-Christian religions also.) 'Give us this day our daily bread, and forgive us our trespasses', we ask, each time that we use the Lord's Prayer. And Jesus Himself prayed on similar lines.[1] Can we devise a theory of prayer – and, more important, can we retain the practice of it – without a belief in a God who acts in the world?

To a surprising extent the answer is 'Yes'. I was taught in boyhood to think of prayer as divided into four or five main sections: adoration, penitence, thanksgiving, and intercession. (The fifth was petition, which was in effect intercession for oneself, and differed from intercession for others in its spiritual role, not in its relationship to the activity of God; it need not, therefore, be treated separately here.) Now of these, adoration is the worship of God for what He is in Himself, quite apart from what He may have done for me and mine: the contemplation and praise of His majesty, beauty, holiness and goodness. And clearly this depends very little on any belief that He acts in specific events in the world. There might be problems over the divine goodness; but even this could be seen in continuist terms. Adoration is explicitly concerned with what God is when we consider Him solely in Himself. There is thus no difficulty for the continuist here, apart from the general standing difficulty of how we know what God is like 'in Himself'.

Penitence similarly. This is concerned partly with contemplation of our own particular selves and their many failings; this of course says nothing about any activity of God's. The other part is prayer to God for forgiveness of those failings. And this certainly asks God to act, but it does not ask Him to act on this world. A penitent criminal may ask God for pardon, believe that pardon has been granted, and yet neither ask nor expect release from prison. Forgiveness is a matter of God's attitude towards me in His heart, and of what I may expect before His judgment-seat; neither of these involve any discontinuity in the world. (Indeed, many would hold that there has been no discontinuity in God's heart either: He has already loved and forgiven, and repentance is really a matter of laying hold of that love and forgiveness in faith and trust.)

What about thanksgiving? Is that affected by our belief or disbelief in God's action in the world? Maybe so, but not so as to rule out all thanksgiving on the part of continuists. They may well thank God for having made the world the way it is, and for its good features – general features, that is, such as beauty, suitability for human life, openness to scientific investigation, and so on. But can they thank God for individual events by which they have been benefited? We might feel that the answer is 'Only if they believe *either* that God deliberately contrived this event for their benefit when designing the original creation – which seems a trifle self-important – *or* that it is an instance of a general feature which He purposed for others as well.' Analogously, I can thank Parliament if it has passed a special private Act for my benefit, or if it has passed a law which is generally valuable, let us say increasing old age pensions, by which I and others will benefit, now or later. But I cannot rationally thank Parliament for increasing pensions if my reason is that this has enabled elderly debtors of mine to pay back what they borrowed from me, for that was not part of Parliament's purpose.

And yet, as we saw earlier (chap. 6, pp. 86-7, above), even this sort of thanks, for an unintended benefit, can make sense. It is a less personal sort of thanks than the usual sort. The usual sort is (in a very small way, perhaps) an expression of love; we are bound closer together by the fact that I have benefited from you and have responded in gratitude. Where the benefit was unintended, the initiative is that of the beneficiary; it is I, who received the good, who choose to make gratitude appropriate, and you, who unintentionally conferred the benefit on me, are only brought into any personal relationship by my action. We have something clearly different from the normal kind of thanksgiving. Nevertheless, it is thanksgiving of a kind; and since God must be presumed at least to have foreseen and welcomed the incidental effects of His plans (where they are good effects, that is), perhaps the initiative is partly His after all.

So far, then, so good. Continuism can retain all of adoration and penitence, and much of thanksgiving. And do not these between them encompass, I will not say the most important parts of the life of prayer, but the holiest parts, the parts most involving the profounder sentiments of the soul? Yet intercession is also part of the traditional Christian prayer-life, as it was of our Lord's own. And can continuism make sense of it?

Some – and by no means all of them continuists – have suggested that the real aim of petitionary prayer is, or ought to be, not so much that God should do what I wish as that I should wish what God does. 'Thy will be done' comes before any petition for ourselves in the Lord's Prayer; 'Not my will, but Thine, be done' was our Lord's own petition in Gethsemane. Even if God does respond to our petitions, it is far more important that we should respond to His will: on fulfilled petitions depend only the comparative trivialities that we think of in time to include them in our prayers, while on a will harmonious with the Lord's depends our sanctification and our glory, and even, it may be, a part of the joy of the Lord Himself.

All this is true, and continuists will very likely accept it. They may hesitate before asking the Lord to make their wills holy, yet may well strive to do it themselves, trying to make their own desires conform to those of the Lord (if they have or think they have some way of telling what those desires are). But this has very little to do with intercession. The most one can say is that if there is good reason to suppose that some event is desired by God, to pray for that event to happen may have the effect of aligning ourselves with His desire; but it seems a curiously roundabout way to achieve this, especially if one is convinced that the literal sense of one's words is quite misguided. To pray for (shall we say) the recovery of a sick friend in the belief that God will not be affected in the slightest by this (apparent) request seems very odd, even if it does have the effect of helping me truly desire the friend's recovery and well-being in the way that the Lord surely does. Of course, it may be that my intercession does affect the Lord in so far as He knows the prayer has been made and approves of it, so that His attitude to me, the intercessor, is altered a little; but not in the sense that it could possibly induce Him to do anything about helping my friend. It seems that intercession is far more self-centred than we had realised; it helps me, but not the friend, which, as I said, seems odd.

Professor Wiles takes the drastic (but logical) step of dismissing *all* prayer for modification of the physical ordering of the world, and confining himself entirely to prayers for grace.[2] Now the obvious objection is that prayers for grace do in fact ask for physical changes (e.g. in the state of my brain). Wiles' rejoinder, that psychological changes need not be brought about by modification of the brain circuits, misses the point; if the change is not brought about by such modifications, *it* will bring *them* about. But he does not really need this rejoinder; for he holds, if I have understood him rightly, that prayer for grace is (a) a means of bringing our lives into relation to some generalised concept of God's will for the world (we can only be more particular about His will with extreme caution), and (b) a part of the search to discern and realise His will for our lives. Even here, then, we are not to pray for any change in the world, even a psychological one. Our words may suggest this; but he seeks to meet the point I raised earlier about the verbal form prayer takes by pointing out that the language of religion habitually uses images to 'make vivid for us the underlying realities of our life'. The hope is simply to be able to use such language 'in a way which does not conflict with other aspects of our understanding of life'.[3] I am not sure whether Wiles realises how drastic the modification of religious language would have to be if his programme were carried out. Surely the effect of current petitionary language would not be to make realities vivid to us but to deceive us into accepting *un*realities. But in any case his argument can be stood on its head. If there is any force at all in what I have been saying in this essay, one 'aspect of our understanding of life' is that it is full of a myriad interactions between persons, human and perhaps divine, and the processes of inanimate nature; in which case it is not the traditional understanding of prayer but Wiles' revisionist version which conflicts with our understanding of life. (The odd thing is that, as we noted earlier, Wiles' own admirable insistence on human freedom has already conceded this point as far as human interaction is concerned. Either 'our understanding of life' really means 'Wiles' theory of how God operates', or Wiles has for the moment forgotten that he is not a full-blooded continuist.)

Wiles, as I said, has no use at all for petitionary prayer, even in a revisionist form, where anything *except* prayer for grace is concerned. (His exegesis of 'Give us this day our daily bread'[4] is more interesting than convincing.) But others have sought to bring the main body of petitionary prayer into a continuist framework. A well-known example some years back was that of Professor D.Z. Phillips in his *The Concept of Prayer*.[5] He begins his chapter on petition by describing what may be called 'superstitious' prayers, prayers lacking any real connection with the life of the person offering the prayer, like the desperate appeal to God of someone in an air-raid. Unless such prayers are followed by a change in the role prayer plays in one's life, Phillips maintains, they are not really religious but superstitious; so far we may agree. But Phillips goes on to suggest that the superstition lies, not (as we might have supposed) in thinking that God may properly be appealed to in urgent need but may equally properly be neglected all our life before and after: no, it lies in using prayer to act on God at all, to influence Him instead of expressing trust in Him like the author of the twenty-third Psalm. The genuinely religious parent of a dying child may say 'O God, let her live!', but this 'is best understood, not as an attempt at influencing the way things go, but as an expression of, and a request for, devotion to God through the way things go.' Believers praying for something are trying to find a meaning and a hope where their desires are so strong that they threaten to destroy that meaning. Of course, Christians have always admitted that every petition must be accompanied by the unspoken but understood clause 'Nevertheless, not what I will, but what Thou wilt'; but for Phillips this clause is the only real prayer. The preceding parts are merely an expression of the 'what I will' which is not to be done unless it happens to be God's will too.

Now Phillips is not trying to set out a new way for the Christian to pray to God. He seriously thinks that he is setting out what the religious believer is doing, and means to be doing, when he or she prays. Yet it seems to me (as I think it has to a good many of Phillips' readers) that the believer normally in fact means what Phillips calls the 'superstitious' element as well as the other one (which is certainly meant to be there also). The most obvious ground for thinking this is one's own notions of what one is doing when one is praying; but another is the fact that the 'Thy will be done' element can be perfectly well expressed, and among the devout usually is, in plain language, side by side with the 'superstitious' prayer, which therefore seems to be something separate from the 'Thy will be done' – and yet used by people who are certainly religious. The only status it has in Phillips' scheme is as an expression of what is threatening the believer's meaning and hope; but why bother to express it? Above all, why express it in the form 'O God, let her live!' when what it means is 'O God, do nothing to let her live unless You were going to do so already'? There are certainly vast differences between an appeal to God and an appeal to the Prime Minister, but on Phillips' view it is hard to see why there should be any at all, even in language. It looks as if Phillips' understanding of prayer has been affected by the common and natural desire of Christians to have it both ways – to insist on the value of prayer and yet not be shaken when prayers seem not to be answered. Most Christians meet this desire by assimilating prayer to some extent to ordinary inter-personal requests: the prayer was not answered because this was not good for us, or not good for some third party, or because intervention in this particular instance would not be appropriate. Phillips, on the other hand, with a more sophisticated philosophical approach, wishes to make all religion (and not just prayer) immune to any criticism from outside. I must say that I do not think this is either possible or desirable.[6]

There is another difficulty we might mention, less basic but still awkward for Phillips. If he is right, should we not be praying as a rule mainly about those things which concern our most urgent desires? And is it not the case that in actual fact a large number of our petitions are about things which are *not* felt all that urgently? We pray for missionaries, say, or for the persecuted, because we are sure that we ought to, not because we are desperately worried by the thought of their troubles and opportunities, so much so as to come close to losing our sense of meaning and hope. (I should add, in fairness, that Phillips does discuss prayer for missionaries. It expresses, he suggests, the meaning prayer has for the praying community and the meaning which belonging to that community has for the person prayed for; while prayer for the conversion of the world may be an expression of the fact that conversion depends on the witness of believers before God, and this in turn on God himself... Even Phillips is a bit doubtful about this.)

The late Professor H.H. Price, who was much more sympathetic to ordinary theism than Phillips is, has also suggested an understanding of prayer which would avoid the need to ask God for discontinuities.[7] That was not, I should add, his aim, though something like it seems to have been in the back of his mind: 'I do not wish to maintain that miracles never happen', he wrote. 'But...they would cease to be miraculous if they happened all day and every day.' How can we avoid this? Well, in the first place we may point to the phenomenon of self-suggestion. When we pray for qualities in ourselves, the prayer may well be 'answered' in this way without any special action by God – indeed, without there necessarily being any God at all. (Conceivably – this is my comment, not Price's – this would fit in with what was said just now about prayer for missions; by praying I stimulate my own concern, and come to give more, or even to go.) But clearly this will not account for all answered prayers. (Price accepts the testimony of William Temple and many other believers that there are enough 'coincidences' in apparent response to prayer for an explanation to be needed.) It is, however, quite possible that there is such a thing as telepathy, operating perhaps by means of a 'common unconscious' which underlies all individual minds. And in that case it might be that the person praying was 'suggesting', not to his or her own self, but to this 'common unconscious'. Hence my prayer for so-and-so to be healed may be transmitted to the medical personnel looking after so-and-so and inspire them to extra zeal and carefulness, God or no God. My prayer would be rather like a broadcast appeal.

Would a theory of this kind be acceptable to continuists? It would require some very serious 'ifs'. We should need to be certain that telepathy existed, for one thing. Also that it was fairly widespread – enough, in our example, to affect the medical team. A telepathic faculty that was very rare would be of little use. And also that it was 'triggered off' in some way by prayer. It is this last that seems hardest to square with continuism (though it is the second that is probably hardest to believe, even for those who think telepathy itself possible or real). For while one can perhaps *imagine* that some future scientific theory will make room both for the processes of nature more or less as we understand them at the present time and for telepathy, without making the latter a discontinuity in the former; still, that such a theory would also allow for prayer to be the best, or even a specially successful way of setting telepathy off, this is surely incredible.

I should add that Price was in most of his essay speaking 'on behalf of' the fool of Psalm 14 who said 'There is no God'; he was trying to see what sense an atheist might make of apparently successful petitionary prayer. When, in his closing paragraphs, he came to ask 'Will it satisfy a religious person who knows by first-hand experience "what it feels like" to pray?' he answers that it will not (except possibly in the case of non-theistic religions like Buddhism). The 'telepathy theory' omits the personal relationship between man and God, the 'I-Thou' element. He is of course quite right. Indeed, this element must be rather embarrassing to continuists. Can one have an 'I-Thou' relationship where the 'Thou' remains wholly passive and silent from start to finish, at least in this life? It does not seem very likely; continuists would probably be better advised to hold that all sense of an 'I-Thou' relationship is delusory, even though the delusion may be spiritually helpful.

Last of all, Price suggested that if we wish to avoid having to accept a constant stream of 'miracles' (as he himself wished, though, as will have been gathered, I see no real difficulty myself), we might say that 'when and if we sincerely place ourselves in this "I-thou" relationship with God, and make our requests to him, the very fact that we do so "releases" paranormal forces of some kind'[8] which bring about the result. Now at first glance this would seem to let in miracle again, just as much as straightforward answer to prayer. The only difference would be that whereas, on the traditional understanding, if I pray for your recovery God answers by healing you, or by inspiring doctors and nurses to do so, on Price's theory He answers by the release of 'paranormal forces' which otherwise would not have been released. And this would be as much a special action by God as the other, except that it brings in forces of which as yet we know nothing, not even that they exist. But if I have understood Price correctly, he is not saying that God releases these forces; they are released by the very fact that I made my request in an 'I-Thou' relationship. God has in fact made it a law of nature (or paranature) that in these circumstances paranormal forces will be released. And this would presumably save continuism, at least a continuism that could stomach paranormal forces in the first place. The trouble is that surely in this case *all* prayers offered in an 'I-Thou' relationship would have to be answered, at least by the release of these forces, and the problem of unanswered prayer would become more acute than ever. If God decides on each request on its merits, then He breaks continuity by releasing the forces; if He does not, then He answers all prayer all the time, or none of it, or according to some rule which has yet to be discovered, but which when discovered would evidently make it possible for one to know which prayers would be answered and which not, and thus to plan one's prayer-life accordingly.[9] None of these seems to me a Christian position; and I feel bound to conclude that Price's suggestions cannot be used to allow a Christian continuist to make room for intercessory prayer.

Notes

1. E.g. Mark 14:36; Luke 22:32; John 17:15; etc.
2. *God's Action in the World*, p. 100
3. Op. cit., p. 106
4. Ibid.
5. London, Routledge, 1965
6. For Phillips' views, see his *Faith and Philosophical Enquiry* (Routledge, 1970); for a critical discussion, Trigg, R., *Reason and Commitment* (Cambridge University Press, 1973), esp. pp. 86 ff.
7. *Essays in the Philosophy of Religion* (Oxford University Press, 1972), p. 45
8. Op. cit., p. 55
9. I suppose it might be that the forces are always released, but are not always adequate to their task. (E.g. the doctors simply do not know enough to be able to cure you, even with the aid of the paranormal forces.) But surely the hypothesis has by now become so complicated as to be incredible?

Guidance

Throughout the history of the Church (and before it) people have been praying to God for guidance, and many have believed that they have received it. When Paul and Silas wanted to go into Asia, and later into Bithynia, the Spirit forbade them; then came the dream of the Macedonian saying 'Come over and help us', and the Apostles took this as guidance.[1] Every minister of the Church of England, before ordination, is asked 'Do you trust that you are inwardly moved by the Holy Ghost to take upon you this Office and Ministry? Do you think that you are truly called, according to the will of our Lord Jesus Christ?' (or, in the Alternative Services Book, 'Do you believe, so far as you know your own heart, that God has called you?') But it is this idea of divine guidance (together with that of providence) which is singled out by Professor Wiles as particularly unjustified. And it will be worth looking at his reason for this. 'The experience of divine guidance or divine providence', he writes, 'is so frequent and so fundamental to Christian experience that if it were to be understood as always implying special divine causation (however possible theoretically that may be), the occurrences of such special divine activity would have to be so numerous as to make nonsense of our normal understanding of the relative independence of causation within the world.'[2]

Now I think we may agree that divine guidance need not always imply special divine causation. Christians have, for instance, long sought guidance from their Bibles or from the sermons and advice of their pastors and friends; and they must frequently have regarded the help they received as a gift from God, although no special divine causation was involved in the particular incident. And we may readily grant that much divine guidance is mediated through other channels as well, as part of God's general provision for His people. Take the sense of 'vocation' to the ordained ministry, already mentioned, where if anywhere we might expect to find signs of guidance (as the Ordinal does). John Newton, in a letter to a young man 'distressed about what was or was not a proper call to the ministry', suggested three signs of such a call: 'a warm and earnest desire to be employed in this service', especially in our best and humblest moments; 'some competent sufficiency as to gifts, knowledge and utterance'; and 'a corresponding opening in Providence, by a gradual train of circumstances pointing out the means, the time, the place, of actually entering upon the work.'[3] It will be generally conceded that the first and second of these can be brought about through perfectly natural means, and entail no special intervention by God; anyone who is going to be a good and worthy minister will desire the work and be fit for it. It is only the third that might make us pause. Obviously a person who finds no opening for ordination will not make a good and worthy minister, for such a person will not become a minister at all. But does that mean that he or she would not have made a good minister if the opening *had* been there? And can the presence of an opening be taken as evidence of guidance or calling unless we suppose that God is specially at work?

In many cases, yes. For the existence or non-existence of such openings is generally in the hands of representatives of Christ's Church, chosen (we hope) for wisdom, piety, virtue, understanding and prudence in such matters; and the exercise of these qualities in a normal and natural way will (we hope) tend to open doors to the worthy and close them to the unworthy. Mistakes will occur from time to time. Jesus Himself chose Judas. But it would be quite possible for God in this way to refrain from giving us direct guidance Himself, and yet to give us fairly reliable (even though fallible) human guides as His agents.

However, although he does not say so, Wiles evidently believes (as a continuist must) that this description applies to *all* cases of guidance. Are there none where we need more? Would it apply, for example, to Paul's journey to Macedonia? This is rather difficult. Luke was perfectly capable of describing people as being prevented by natural or human means from doing something;[4] here, therefore, he is surely speaking of the Holy Spirit as directly at work in preventing the Apostles from going into Asia or Bithynia. Paul and his companions clearly took the same view of the dream, though a continuist could no doubt urge that this was either coincidence or Paul's subconscious at work. Right or wrong, the Bible here evidently says that God was directly at work. And many subsequent accounts of guidance take the same line. When St Augustine heard the voice calling '*Tolle, lege*', his first reaction was to wonder whether this was just part of a normal children's game, and only when he found himself unable to think of any game which involved those words did he go and look at his Paul, deciding that the voice must have come from God.[5] Right or wrong, he believed that it was, shall we say, more appropriate for God to bring him to the last step into faith by calling to him specially than to do so by coincidence.

But of course Luke, Paul and Augustine may have judged wrongly, not rightly. Consider Wiles' point about the excessive frequency of the experience of divine guidance. As a matter of fact, I doubt if he is really right here, even if every claim to divine guidance did also entail a claim to special divine causation (and we have seen that it does not). Even the most saintly do not, I think, claim divine guidance for every moment of their lives; most would say it had happened on only a few occasions. And this would hardly be enough to 'make nonsense' of our normal understanding of cause and effect. Ideas come into our minds dozens of times a day; divine guidance, even including those forms of it which we have agreed do not call for special divine action, form only a small part of these – shall we be generous and say one in a thousand? And since only ideas in our minds (or events leading to such ideas) are usually reckoned instances of guidance, all other events leave our notions of cause and effect untouched (unless, of course, we have other reasons for believing there to be interventions in the world of nature, which in some cases, I have been arguing, we do). The proportion of actual instances of guidance in the life of the individual (let alone the history of the universe) is tiny, and we may readily concede that many even of these are instances of *general* guidance, not of special divine causation, and may be left out of account. The result is that our total picture of the world is hardly affected at all. Even supposing that every single Christian believes himself or herself to be directly guided by God once a week, how big a proportion is this of the number of thoughts that they have and the number of happenings that befall them? 'One in a thousand' is beginning to look far too high a figure. If they have only one thought or idea a minute for sixteen hours a day, 'guidance' would form one sixty-seventh of one per cent of those thoughts; and this only for human beings among all the higher animals, and maybe only for the Christians among them at that.

Honesty obliges me to concede that if the case I have been trying to make out in the preceding chapters of this essay is a sound one, there are many more discontinuities in the world than just the cases of alleged special divine guidance. Though most of them are part of a system of cause and effect, it is neither a materialist system nor a determinist one. If Wiles' 'normal understanding' is materialist or determinist – which I am sure it is not – then it does need to be made nonsense of. But this means that continuists are faced with an awkward choice. If they take their stand on guidance alone, this is too rare to disturb our notions of cause and effect; but if they allow into the debate all the other instances of discontinuity for which I have been arguing, the disturbance of these notions is indeed somewhat greater, but it is supported by far stronger evidence.

Nevertheless, I am inclined to think that this is probably the one area, of all those we have been surveying or shall survey, where the continuists come nearest to having a plausible case. I do not think they are right even here; but this is not because I can prove that the idea of special intervening guidance is absolutely necessary to any Christian view-point, but because their case is so weak on the other points that there seems no positive reason to accept it here, where it is stronger. It is stronger here simply because of the manifest existence of what I have called 'general guidance', guidance through already existing agents, and the difficulty of showing that any one given example of guidance does not come under that heading. In order to show this we should have to do one of two things. One would be to show that the natural circumstances of the case were insufficient to produce the 'guidance'. Now our knowledge is obviously nowhere near enough to enable us to do any such thing. Moreover, if human decisions and thoughts in general are not always wholly predetermined by natural circumstances (as I have claimed earlier), then the apparently guided ones aren't either; and in that case our knowledge could never, even in principle, be enough to show that the natural circumstances plus indeterminism were inadequate to produce the 'guidance'; only that by themselves they did not make it probable. The other possible approach would be to show that in an alleged case of special guidance the guidance was so vital to God's purposes that He could not possibly have left it to 'general guidance'. But this again seems to be something one could never prove for certain.

We may, then, allow that if continuism were plausible in all other areas, the evidence for special divine guidance would not be enough to disprove it. But then I do not think it *is* plausible in all other areas, and I hope that the reader will agree.

Notes

1. Acts 16:6-10
2. *The Remaking of Christian Doctrine*, pp. 37-8
3. *Select Letters of John Newton* (London, Banner of Truth, 1960), pp. 54-5
4. See e.g. Luke 5:19; Acts 19:30, 27:12 ff.
5. *Confessions* VIII, 29

Grace

It might be thought that in accounting – or trying to account – for God's grace continuists would be on their weakest ground. The whole idea of grace is surely that of an influence upon us from above, from beyond us, an intervention which moves us or empowers us in a way that we should never have moved or empowered ourselves. 'Not I, but the grace of God working in me'[1] has surely been the experience of innumerable Christians, not just of St Paul.

Yet continuists can make a surprisingly strong defence of their position. Is it not true (they might say) that the root of the idea of God's grace is the idea of His *graciousness*, the sheer kindness of God towards us? When Paul says 'where sin abounded, grace did much more abound',[2] he is not surely speaking of individual acts of God's intervention occurring to affect the world, any more than he is speaking of individual acts that happen to be sinful: he is concerned with the terrible spread of sinfulness over all the human world, and the glorious kindness of God that is greater even than that. And God's kindness is all about us. 'We bless thee for our creation, preservation, and all the blessings of this life,' says a well-known prayer. Assuredly this is God being gracious to us and yet these things do not call for any miraculous interference on His part.

Nor is it otherwise if we think of that grace which is God's kindness enabling us to do good. Calvinist theologians (I am not sure whether the expression is to be found in Calvin himself) have traditionally spoken of God's 'common grace', that which restrains the evil effects of sin and enables even the unregenerate to do acts of 'civic righteousness', acts that are righteous in the eyes of other people though defective, and therefore sinful, in those of the Lord. And this common grace is meted out to us, not by miracle, but through the ordinances of everyday life: through the influence of the law, of teachers, of family upbringing, even of the Christian message in so far as it is recognised as wise in ethics, though not yet as God's news of salvation. It reaches us through natural means; the closed web is not disturbed. And yet it is certainly grace.

Is it, then, only *saving* grace which requires special divine action? But does even this do so? The General Thanksgiving I quoted just now goes on to praise God for 'the means of grace' – that is, above all, for the Word and the Sacraments, though doubtless other things too, such as the Church herself, are included. Now whatever the *origins* of the Word and the Sacraments may be, they come to us now by natural means within the closed web. My Bible was printed, bound, published and sold like any other book. The water of Baptism is natural water. The bread and wine used in the Holy Communion were baked and fermented in the normal way. (It is true that those who believe in 'transubstantiation' have been known to call this a miracle. But if it is one, it is a queer kind of miracle, one which leaves the web as undisturbed as if there had been no miracle at all: cause and effect follow their usual pattern.)

Now if God's kindness in creating and preserving us, and His kindness in enabling us to do good, and even His kindness in the 'means of grace' – if all these are given to us with no disruption of the world's continuity, then surely the general concept of divine grace requires no such disruption, and the continuist may believe in grace as fully and sincerely as the rest of us, and with no inconsistency. 'Many factors, not of my doing,' writes Professor Wiles, 'have come together and impinged on me at that moment' (that is, of my conversion), 'and it is these that I acknowledge as the "Not I" of my conversion and ascribe with gratitude to the grace of God.'[3] Of course, those who are not continuists may believe, if they wish, that there are also special acts of God's grace, that from time to time He touches people's hearts in ways that have their source in His intervention, not in the normal sequence of events. But they cannot surely believe that all God's kindness is displayed in this manner; they must admit that in many cases only natural events are involved, and yet His grace is at work; and therefore they must admit that a continuist who accepts the reality of these cases and their ultimate origin in God is as genuine a believer in grace as they themselves are. The special stress laid on grace in Christian belief has arisen chiefly from the conviction that God is a God of love, and from the conviction that it is not we ourselves who have any hope of saving ourselves. But these are preserved in the continuist's view of grace as strongly as in anybody else's. God's love has filled His creation with means of grace: and left to my own devices, that is, without Bible or Church or Sacraments, I should be hopelessly lost. It is still God's kindness that saves me, though it is a kindness which is there, built into the foundations of the universe, not one that steps in to pick me out – and leave others lost.

Not that continuism has to be Pelagian! It is indeed true that Pelagius himself and maybe a good many of his succesors, have, consciously or unconsciously, taken a rather 'continuist' view of grace. It has been said of Pelagius that to him God's grace embraced His endowment of mankind with free will, the law of Moses, the forgiveness of sins through the death of Christ, the example of Christ, and the teaching of Christ. And all these things can operate on the soul without infringing continuity (though I should myself deny that they could come into being in the first place without infringing it). But the fact that Pelagius was (in this respect) something of a continuist does not mean that continuists have to be Pelagians. Professor Wiles' version of 'Not I...' is hardly Pelagian. One might indeed argue that continuism has one important feature in common with Augustine, and an embarrassing feature at that. For in holding (as did Augustine) that all movement towards good in the soul is by the power of God, continuists are faced with the objection that in that case all movement towards evil must also be by the power of God (or at least by His withholding of His power) and then how do we avoid making God the author of sin? Of course, both have answers to this. Wiles insists very strongly on human freedom: God has 'conferred on parts at least of his creation a genuine independence of agency in relation to himself'.[4] And the Augustinians could point out that precisely because they believe that movements towards good are miraculous acts of divine grace, whereas movements towards evil are not miraculous at all, there is a clear sense in which for them God is the author of good in a way in which He is *not* the author of evil.

For many in the Augustinian tradition would, I think, wish to say that saving grace not only often is, but always *has* to be, a miracle. I have already mentioned how Augustine himself seems to have felt that if the call '*Tolle, lege*' had been part of a normal children's game it could not have been a message from God. I have, too, on my shelves a small devotional work on the words of Christ from the Cross, in which the author suggests that the unpromising background of the penitent thief's conversion was intended 'to teach us that every genuine conversion is the direct product of the *supernatural* operation of the Holy Spirit'.[5] Must this indeed be so? If it must, then clearly continuists are in an impossible situation; they have ruled out salvation altogether, or obliged themselves to deny that we are saved by grace.

But ought one to assert that the supernatural operation of the Spirit is always necessary? It could be because this seems to be the only way in which one could say 'Not I, *nor anyone nor anything else*, but the grace of God working in me.' To ascribe to a created person or object the power to convert or save (even if that power is ultimately derived from God) is intolerable. Yet continuists might reasonably point out that on any view God very rarely converts and saves by *pure* miracle. He uses created means; things like a preacher, a copy of the Bible, a child's voice, a passage from Luther's preface to Romans. Even the penitent thief was converted by words spoken in a human voice. If, then, it is certain that God converts by means of such things, why insist that He must always use a miracle as well? Or rather, conversely, if He has to use supernatural means, and cannot save us without them, why does He bother to use natural ones as as well? He would be like a doctor who knew that a certain drug, and only that one, would cure a certain disease, yet who always prescribed other medicines as well, even whilst well aware that they were quite useless and unnecessary.

Is it, perhaps, a question of one's view of human nature? Continuists may urge that God's lovingkindness is there, supernatural operation or no supernatural operation, and that human knowledge of that lovingkindness may be there also, learnt by way of 'natural' means (including the reading of Scripture and hearing the preaching of the Word). Human response to knowledge of that lovingkindness, though it will have supernatural results, is in itself just that, a human response, and to that extent 'natural' once again. All may be present without a special operation of the Holy Spirit, and there is no need of such an operation for God to produce a genuine conversion. (Perhaps the story of the penitent thief was included in order to show that there can also be conversion by supernatural means? – but that is a discontinuist suggestion.) But all this seems to imply that it is possible for us to respond to God's lovingkindness without divine aid. And we may hold that this is *not* possible, simply because human nature is fallen. A purely human response (human in its cause, that is, as well as in its context) would be infected with sin and quite incapable of doing the work necessary for conversion. The fact that God is the ultimate cause of this response (as of everything else) is beside the point: the *immediate* causes of this response are infected with sin.

Others will not be happy with this. Acceptance of mercy is not a 'work' at all; no-one praises me for having received a Christmas-present, or lists it among my creditable acts. 'There will be few so foolish as to assert that a poor man does a good work if he comes in his poverty to receive a gift from the hand of a rich,' said Luther.[6] Moreover, however the Holy Spirit brings about our response to grace, even if He does so by direct action, that response remains the response of a sinner; if He does so indirectly, or leaves the response to human free will, the response is still the acceptance of God's mercy and love. Either way, the initiative is divine; either way, the response is human.

There is something in this. But what does this 'initiative'

amount to? If we allow special divine actions, it could take one of two forms. It could be a direct 'supernatural operation'; or it could be an *indirect* one. It is interesting to read, for example, C.S. Lewis' *Surprised by Joy*[7] with the present discussion in mind. The means whereby Lewis came to faith did not seem supernatural; certainly they did not seem to involve a direct operation of the Holy Spirit upon him. They were chiefly literary and personal influences – George MacDonald, G.K. Chesterton, George Herbert, and his friends Tolkien and Dyson. Yet he had no doubt that God was 'behind' all this, and not just in the sense of having created the world in which these influences existed. The language he uses to describe the process is that of a fish being caught by an angler, a chessplayer being defeated, a fox being hunted (he felt himself to be a most unwilling convert!). There was, or seemed to be, a personal element involved on the divine side as well as on the human; there was a Person at work, and not just a natural process. (He may, of course, have been wrong.) It looks as if God were operating, not by overwhelming the mind of His 'quarry', nor by leaving nature to take its course, but by planting ideas in that mind, and in those of people he knew – even in 'one of the hardest-boiled atheists I ever knew', who never afterwards showed the slightest interest in Christianity. The final collapse of resistance and the last stages that preceded it, may in this view have been 'natural', following on (with due allowance for human freedom) from previous stages; but the initiative in bringing those previous stages about belonged to God. Here we would have, then, an *indirect* supernatural operation; and the conversion is as genuine as one where the operation was direct. It is just as clearly 'not I, but the grace of God' at work.

Now is this so in conversion as described by Professor Wiles? Here the divine initiative is restricted to the creation of the universe in the first place. Unless the form that creation took was planned with my conversion in mind, there is scarcely more reason to say 'Not I, but the grace of God' about my conversion than about my coming to prefer my tea without sugar. ('Scarcely more', not 'no more'; God may have had conversions generally in mind when He made the worlds, although not mine in particular.) And let us remember that continuists have to do more than assert that God can save by wholly 'natural' means of grace. They have to deny that there was anything but fortunate coincidence in (say) the processes that led up to Lewis' conversion. They have, moreover, to hold that in all cases where a convert believes that God has been specially at work on him or her (as in Lewis' case, or those of Paul or Augustine) this is a complete mistake, and that any special love or gratitude that arises in response to this belief is unwarranted.

Professor Wiles has not of course overlooked this argument. 'Read such stories forwards instead of retrospectively and there is no escape,' he answers, 'from the arbitrary election, implausible disposition of external circumstances, and unacceptable manipulation of inner life.'[8] One is tempted to say 'implausible to, and unacceptable by, whom?' Not Paul or Augustine, clearly; they actually believed in the dispositions and welcomed the manipulations. The 'arbitrary election' is a more serious point, one must agree; but the difficulties in this idea are not new, nor have they gone unmet in the course of the development of Christian theology. And certainly what we are offered instead is – to me – much more implausible and unacceptable than anything Paul or Augustine believed about their conversions. The world God made, we are told, 'includes as a paramount part of its purpose the self-dedication of human lives such as those of a Paul or an Augustine'.[9] It may, indeed, I believe it does. But I believe this, partly because the accounts Paul and Augustine give of what led to that self-dedication seem plausible and acceptable to me, as they do not to Wiles, and partly because of what is given in what I, but not Wiles, believe to be God's revelation. Paul and Augustine were certainly produced as part of the world God has made. But then so were Bobby Jones and Henry Cotton; so, for that matter, were Caligula and Stalin. Why not suppose that skill at golf, or tyranny, were paramount parts of God's purpose?

Perhaps this is not quite fair. Continuists do not deduce God's purposes from the lives of Paul and Augustine; they think that they know those purposes already, and can see that the saints' lives fit in with them. But there are other difficulties. For one thing, it seems no special gratitude is due from the convert to God for his or her salvation – at best, the sort of gratitude which we thought of earlier, which can thank a stranger for geraniums in their window-box. It was part of God's plan that some people should dedicate themselves to Him; it was no part of it that *I* should, or Paul or Augustine should. God's kindness is general, not particular. It is not merely that He does not love me more than he does so-and-so. That is fair enough; who am I that the Lord should pick me out? It is, rather, that He does not love *either* me or so-and-so, except in general terms. What happens to either of us as individuals is to Him apparently a matter of indifference; I can be *pleased* if I am saved, but hardly *grateful*.

Equally unwarranted, of course, is any sense of *assurance*. The Calvinist believes 'God has elected me, and He will not let me go.' The Arminian believes 'Grace has reached me, and only my own defection can undo its work.' But the continuist believes 'I have been at the receiving end of a fortunate chain of events which has led me to faith in Christ; but I have no reason to suppose that I may not shortly be at the end of another, less fortunate chain of events which will lead me to lose that faith.' All three must, of course, live with the knowledge that backsliders do exist. But at least Arminians can feel sure that 'it will only be by my own fault that I become one of their number', and even Calvinists can be sure that if their conversions were real in the first place they will never be undone. Continuists have the worst of both worlds. Their conversion may be real enough, but it may be undone, as it was brought about, by something that is neither their own work nor the reprobation of God, but simply the fortuitous workings of the universe. 'Not I, but...' takes on a grimmer note. This may be the truth, and therefore to be faced resolutely; but if it is, it is a miserable sort of truth, and not what one expects from the Christian gospel.

I can see one way in which continuists might try to retain gratitude and assurance in spite of what I have been saying. That is by adopting Universalism, and holding that God's purpose is to save *all* people. For if this is God's purpose, then I can certainly be grateful to Him for it, whatever the means may be by which He brings me to the common destiny; and of course if I can be sure that everyone will be saved, I know that I shall be among them. But do continuism and Universalism really go together very well? Universalists, as I understand it, have usually believed that God would eventually, if not in this life then in the next, coax, press or otherwise draw each and every soul away from sin and self and towards repentance and Himself. The picture is throroughly discontinuist; one might say, even more so than more orthodox views, as God goes on intervening until His goal is reached. A continuist Universalism would have, I think, to suppose something like this: God creates a world constructed somehow in such a way that there is a certain chance of a given person reaching salvation in a given period of time. ('World' here, of course, includes the 'next world' as well as this one.) As time passes, the chance that any one person has held out in sin and unbelief grows steadily smaller, and as there is a finite number of people to be saved, after a time there is only a negligible chance that *anyone* is left outside heaven. If continuists wish to hold this sort of view, I am not sure that they can be refuted. What I am sure of is that they have no *reason* to hold it. It is certainly without Biblical support, even in those passages most suggesting Universalism; for these link the larger hope, not to the construction of the universe, but to the Cross of Christ.[10] And it is also without empirical support from what we see in the world. There are many people who come to God; there are also many who turn (or drift) away from Him; there are many who never seem to have a 'live option' of doing either. Can it really be supposed that we have enough evidence to say that God has created the sort of world in which everyone is virtually bound to be saved in the end – and say this about a world to come of which we have no experience, but which is undoubtedly very different from *this* world in many important ways? If any continuists really wish to hold the position I have been describing – whether any do, I do not know – they can only do so by treating Universalism in the same way as they treat traditionally orthodox Christianity: that is, by abandoning so much of it that, even if there was some reason to believe elements of the usual version true, there is certainly none to believe the continuist one.

What are we to say, then, about the initially quite strong case that continuists seemed to be able to make out for themselves where grace was concerned? This, I think: if God does act specially from time to time, if there really are cases of extraordinary, supernatural grace reaching out and touching people, then we may well believe that He also works through natural means to the same end (always remembering that behind those 'natural' means there probably lie supernatural origins). Given that the Lord really did set out to convert Paul or Augustine, I may then have good reason to believe that lives dedicated to Him are part of His paramount purpose, however their dedication is brought about. And therefore I may accept (unless I have other reasons to reject it) the account the continuist gives of more 'natural' conversions. But I must have some evidence, in revelation or experience, my own or other people's, for believing that the Lord is a God of grace in the first place. Most Christians believe that they have this; but then most Christians are not continuists.

Notes

1. I Corinthians 15:10
2. Romans 5:20
3. *God's Action in the World*, p. 76
4. Ibid., pp. 20-1
5. Pink, A.W., *The Seven Sayings of the Saviour on the Cross* (Grand Rapids, Baker, 1976), p. 30
6. 'The Pagan Servitude of the Church' in *Selected Writings*, ed. Dillenberger, J. (New York, Doubleday, 1961), p. 286
7. London, Bles, 1955
8. Wiles, op. cit., p. 81
9. Ibid.
10. E.g. I Corinthians 15:22, I Timothy 2:4-6

Revelation

It has already been argued[1] that natural theology by itself will not give us even a minimally Christianised deism. It may yield the existence of a First Cause and source of order (though many deny even this); it may just possibly yield that of a power working for good. It will not yield that of a God of love; for the being it indicates may be utterly impersonal, and the good he or it works for might include the annihilation of mankind for their sins. Of course, the natural theologian may go on to argue that the closest analogy we have to this sort of being seems to be the human mind, with its powers of creativity and imagination: in the former we have the imposition of new kinds of order on the world, and in the latter, in the framing of mental images for instance, something curiously close to creation *ex nihilo*. But not only is this an argument from analogy, and a very tenuous analogy at that, to the extent that it is valid, it describes the life of the Deity as analogous to some of the most 'discontinuous' aspects of human life. Much of living is automatic, following patterns of which we are largely unconscious; it is precisely in our moments of creativity and imagination that we most seem to break free from this.

However this may be, something more than natural theology seems to be needed if mankind is to know anything worthwhile about God. Certainly this is so if our continuism is to be a *Christian* continuism. For the Christian theologian, however unorthodox, not only stands but *wants* to stand in the succession of Christian teaching which goes back to the Bible. However loosely he sits with regard to the biblical tradition, there has to be some account given of it, some justification for his position in it; the natural line to take is that in or behind the Bible lies something which can be called, in some sense or other, the revelation of God.

Moreover, there is at least one major Christian belief, not about God but about ourselves, which it is difficult to hold without relying on revelation – namely, belief in life after death. There have indeed been many attempts to prove on a basis of reason alone that life continues after we die, from Plato to McTaggart, but it is many years since any of these have found much favour among either philosophers or theologians. (It is, of course, hard to fit such arguments in with a belief in God's omnipotence; if God is almighty, He can annihilate us, and reason alone can surely never show that He doesn't.) Certainly I know of no Christian continuist who uses such arguments. Surely any belief in a future life rests, and must rest, upon an assurance from God; that is, upon revelation. (Unless, indeed, it is based upon the evidence adduced by psychical research. This is in effect a kind of revelation from finite sources, the spirits, it is alleged, of the departed, or the experiences of those who have temporarily 'died' and bring back memories of a continued existence. Neither of these, I should have thought, is any more acceptable to continuists than revelation from God.)

We might add, perhaps, that natural theology by itself would be a very unsuitable vehicle for conveying the truths of religion, which, if they are truths at all, are the most important truths in the world. For natural theology is by its nature confined to an intellectual élite, and those who are not equipped to follow its arguments, or who do not know what these are, cannot even accept their validity on trust as they may the results of scientists or historians, since there is notoriously no agreement about natural theology even within this élite. If people generally are to know anything about God, something more is surely required; and that something is usually taken to be revelation.

Now the word 'revelation' may be understood in rather different ways according to whether it is the divine giving or the human receiving of it that we have in mind. I think that as far as the former is concerned, it might be defined as any act of God whereby knowledge is acquired by us. For it has been customary to distinguish between a general or natural revelation on the one hand, and special revelation(s) on the other; yet both originate in God's activity. The former clearly can originate in activity which in no way breaks the continuity of the universe. 'Ever since the world was created the invisible qualities of God, his eternal power and deity, have been perceived in the things He has made,' wrote St Paul.[2] Not in special acts, in miracles or prophecies for example, but in the ordinary processes of nature. There is no disagreement here (except on the part of those who deny that there is a such a thing as general revelation, and I have no intention of trying to defend that view). But it differs from natural theology only in being, as it were, seen from God's point of view, as flowing from His creative action; it has much the same disadvantages.

The problem arises, of course, when we come to consider alleged cases of special revelation. Here we may make one concession to the continuist. There has been serious distortion of the idea of revelation by the tendency of many Christians to assimilate it all to one particular kind of revelation, namely prophecy. The prophets believed that they were specially and directly given messages from God, and the command to utter them. But the very fact that a large part of Scripture is prophetical should warn us that other parts are *not* – just as the very fact that some parts of the prophetical books are accounts of visions should warn us that other parts aren't. We must not treat the authors of (say) the Book of Ezra or the Acts of the Apostles as prophets, nor suppose that the Spirit of God must have worked through them in the same way as He did through Amos or Jeremiah. Perhaps this is best illustrated by pointing to the 'wisdom' books of the Old Testament. There was a great deal of 'wisdom' circulating in Israel (and outside). Solomon is said to have been wiser than Ethan the Ezrahite and Heman, Calcol and Darda, the sons of Mahol;[3] but he differed from them, one presumes, in degree rather than kind. His wisdom was an *enduring* gift from the Lord, not a series of separate bits of wise judgment placed in his mind when needed; it was 'a heart wise and understanding'[4] that he asked for and was given, not a constant stream of supernatural advice. Many of his proverbs were never included in the Book of Proverbs (whereas some from non-Israelite sources *were*); yet there is no reason to suppose that his 'biblical' proverbs were a product of his divine gift and his other ones were not. (To be fair, the same applies to the prophets.) Again, there were many things which our Lord Himself said and did during His life on earth which were not incorporated into the Gospels,[5] and which were nevertheless the words and deeds of God incarnate. Surely we are not to see the Evangelists as getting a second lot of inspiration over and above His for their work in recording (as opposed to their work in editing and commenting) but rather to see them as channels for those revelations in the deeds and words of Jesus Christ which God wished to be preserved for us. In neither wisdom nor Gospel-writing was the kind of inspiration associated with prophecy involved.

But can we go farther than this, and assimilate all alleged revelation to the insight of the 'wise' and then make this in turn a normal (though doubtless rare and valuable) part of continuous nature? 'Inspiration', wrote T.H. Sprott at the beginning of this century, 'is not the direct communication of knowledge to the human mind: it is power of insight, so that he perceives the Divine meaning in Nature or Conscience or History, which though always there and always appealing, had been before un-perceived.'[6] Now I cannot myself think that this is correct. And even if it were, it would not be enough to give us a tenable continuist theory of revelation. I have already set out the main reasons for thinking this in chapter 5, but it might be worthwhile going over them again, in a little more detail.

Firstly, there is the matter of what the prophets themselves said. It could be that the authors of Job or Kings did write as they did because of insight into the divine meaning of nature, conscience and history. But over and over again the prophets claim, *not* insight, but 'direct communication of knowledge' from the Lord. They may of course have been deluded; but that suggests, not the possession of unusual insight, but a serious lack of it in the understanding even of what was going on in their own minds. It is not easy to accept the content of their prophecies as authoritative insight, and yet refuse to accept their statements about how that content came to them. Professor Wiles, indeed, replying to a similar point raised by Professor Mitchell, argued that few accept the full details of everything the inspired writers said. Mark portrays Jesus as victor over the demons, and this in cases which we should be inclined to label 'epilepsy'. If Mark was wrong on this point, might not the prophets be wrong in claiming direct communication from God, and yet be possessed of the superior religious insight usually ascribed to them?[7]

They might. But there is surely a difference between the two kinds of error. If a spy claims to have good information about enemy dispositions, the fact that he has some mistakes does not invalidate his claim. But if he says that he took his notes from the enemy general's personal papers, and there is proof that he didn't, serious doubt is cast on his reliability as a whole.

Moreover, the notion of 'insight' is a vague one and hard to pin down. There is the insight of the fictional detective, who fits together a series of apparently unconnected clues sprinkled through the pages of the book and shows that these point inevitably to such-and-such a conclusion. There is the insight of the scientist who realises that a certain hypothesis will account for the known facts; or of the critic who sees how it was that the artist or poet achieved a certain effect; or of the textual scholar who suddenly spots an emendation which will make sense of what a hitherto unintelligible manuscript reads. And of course there is the insight of the wise friend or pastor who knows me well and can understand my troubles and my joys, helping me to bear the one and sharing with me in the other. Now I can see that something like this might be ascribed to the Biblical writers in some instances. Perhaps God's hand in the workings of the universe is analogous to that which is seen by the detective or the scientist. But if insight into it is soundly and logically based, we ought surely to prefer it set out in logical form, so that we may follow the reasoning of our spiritual detectives and scientists. The prophets ought to have been theologians. On the other hand, if their insight was more akin to an 'intelligent guess', or even if it was some special faculty of theirs, we ought to be able to check it. (Did the accused break down and admit guilt, or, quite the other way, produce an unbreakable alibi? Does the hypothesis suggest a test experiment, and if so, what is the result?) Either way, we may *start* with 'insight', but what we want in the end is something stronger than that, a humanly devised proof or test (notoriously very hard to get in questions of religion). Are we back at the demand for natural theology once more?

Of course, it may be answered that the same holds true for *any* theory of revelation. Suppose that all the Bible was literally dictated by the Holy Spirit. Should we not even then need to check its claims in some way or another, in order to find out whether it really had been so dictated? After all, similar claims might be made – indeed *are* made – for the Koran and the Book of Mormon. Does allowing that a revelatory act may lie behind the prophet's oracle make it any more deserving of belief than if it were simply a matter of his or her insight into the divine meaning of nature, conscience or history?

Yes: for two reasons. The first is the more important in principle, though the less so in practice. A claim to particular insight into the divine meaning of an event must stand or fall by its own merits. If, let us say, Isaiah claims to see in the advance of the Assyrian army the rod of the Lord's anger,[8] we can only judge the probability of such a claim in the light of Judah's sins, the effects of invasion, what we know of the character of the Lord from other sources, the success of any previous insights Isaiah may have claimed – that sort of thing. If, however, Isaiah claims, not insight, but a word from the Lord, then while these criteria remain relevant, we have an additional reason which might incline us to accept what he says, namely, the possibility that God, whose word can be trusted, really is the ultimate source of the oracle. Moreover, there could in theory be external evidence suggesting that the oracle was indeed divine revelation – e.g. the theophany at Mount Sinai and its sequels in the history of prophecy (including Isaiah's own call). In principle, as I said, this is very important indeed: the insights of wise but fallible men and women may clash and contradict one another, but the oracles of a God of truth will not. In practice, unfortunately, it is not so important, because of the existence of false prophets and competing claims to divine inspiration.

The second reason is this: Insights stand, to a great extent, alone. As I said just now, the insights of the wise may clash: and some may be right and others wrong, even where only one wise person is concerned. If Isaiah sees Assyria as the rod of the Lord's anger, and is right to do so, this has very little connection with his other insight that the invaders will not capture Jerusalem;[9] one might be true and the other mistaken. The independence is not of course complete. The second 'insight' would depend to some extent on the first, combined with the widespread belief, itself depending on the insights of earlier sages, that Jerusalem was the especial city and dwelling-place of the Lord. On the other hand, prophets do not stand alone; still less do the oracles of any one individual prophet. Each is part of a sequence sent (it is alleged) by the Lord; each therefore has his or her credibility increased by the credibility of the others; which is not so with the insights of the wise. We do not trust the judgment of Socrates more because of the existence of Confucius.

But even supposing that assimilation of prophecy to wisdom were possible, can a Christian continuist theory of revelation be based even on wisdom? Arguments related to those we have been considering suggest that it cannot. The Wisdom books proper of the Bible are to a large extent summaries or distillations of the experience of generations of believers. Their truth can therefore be recognised by many; we might never have thought of what they say for ourselves, but when we read or hear it, we realise its weight and its worth. This is in fact Professor Wiles' position in the article quoted above. He compares the insight of the inspired writers to that of an 'inspired' art critic, whose comments on a painting cannot be compared with what the actual painter says, because the painter is dead, but they do enable us to see features of the painting which we should not otherwise have seen.

But this does not apply to the prophets. Insight into the divine meaning of conscience or nature finds an echo, it may be, in our own experience of conscience and nature. (Wiles' critic is much closer in insight to the *scientist* than the religious teacher; the scientist really does discern patterns in the universe – put there by God, we believe – which we should not have seen, but which, in some cases anyway, we can recognise for ourselves afterwards.) Insight into the divine meaning of history – and this was the special field of the prophets – is another matter altogether. If the oracles of the prophets are insights at all, they are insights which we are unable even to follow; we must take them on trust from the élite who have them. The prophets become, not humble mouthpieces of the Deity, but super-philosophers with strange powers of penetration which we can only admire in ignorance, or reject. And one wonders whether this is really an accurate picture of them.

In any case, human wisdom – even that which is embodied in the Bible – is inadequate as a vehicle for God's revelation. It can help; it cannot be all. 'In the wisdom of God', said St Paul, 'the world did not know God through wisdom';[10] and even in the wisdom books themselves this is in effect admitted. Eliphaz the Temanite and Bildad the Shuhite and Zophar the Naamathite were 'wise'; and no doubt, as Job said with bitterness, wisdom would perish with them.[11] But their wisdom is nothing, indeed it is perverse, in the face of the Lord speaking out of the whirlwind; they had not spoken what was right of Him, as Job had who asked questions rather than giving the answers. The Lord who acts and intervenes is more than all insight. And without such action and intervention, the waters of wisdom run slowly out in the desert of Ecclesiastes: 'in much wisdom is much vexation, and he who increases knowledge increases sorrow'.[12] 'Such', wrote Charles Williams, 'beyond the prophets, is the undertone of man's knowledge; such is the wise man's judgment... Ecclesiastes spoke of what he knew, and of what many millions of others have known after him.'[13] Insight discloses that insight is not enough.

Wisdom runs dry because the fountain needs to be replenished. If it is to convey knowledge about that which is more than human, it must have something to work on which is more than just the product of human thought. To distil the experience of generations and get truth about God from it, that experience must not be limited to experience of the universe, untouched by God since the creation. Nor can we discern the divine meaning in nature, conscience and history unless first of all we know, somehow, that there *is* a meaning to be discerned, and have some sort of clue as to what 'divine' may mean – what, in fact, God, or God's purposes, may be like. And this has to come from Him, either by His acting in the world to tell us, or by His enabling our insight to see beyond the universe; both of which, if indeed they can be distinguished, break that universe's continuity.

So far, of course, we have been taking it for granted that revelation, whether in wisdom or in prophecy, is a matter of truths and propositions. But in speaking of insight seeing beyond the universe, we have let in another possibility. Has not much discussion of revelation in recent years concentrated, after all, on that which is *not* propositional? With one suggested alternative to the propositional, to wit, the suggestion that the Bible is the human record of *acts* of God in which He revealed Himself to His people, we are not here concerned. True, partially true, or false, it is an unacceptable suggestion as far as the continuist is concerned, as unacceptable as the crudest fundamentalism. According to continuism, we cannot know of God through His acts in history and record them; we can only call certain events in history His acts because we already (somehow) know His nature or purposes. But what of the view that revelation is primarily not of facts but of a Person? 'What is offered to man's apprehension', wrote William Temple, 'in any specific revelation is not truth concerning God but the living God himself';[14] and of course this thought is biblical enough, in its positive assertion at least. 'The only-begotten God, who is in the bosom of the Father, he has revealed him'.[15] Now I do not myself think that the propositional element can be eliminated.

It can and should be regarded as less than the personal element; no knowledge *about* God can possibly substitute for the knowledge face to face that we long for; nor even for puzzling reflections in a mirror such as we may hope for in this life. But it seems absurd to say that we know nothing about God unless we know Him personally; and if we do know Him personally, knowledge about Him follows automatically. However, even if I am quite mistaken here, we are no nearer a continuist theory of revelation. There is more, not less, discontinuity in the revealing of God himself than in the revealing of truths about Him. For at least the truths *are* truths, and to that extent resemble those truths which we know by other means than revelation. We know and believe many facts and propositions; this kind of revelation simply adds to our store, or that which was there already. But the revealing of God himself is quite another matter. If that takes place, it must needs be something unlike, and greater than, anything else that can happen in our lives, even revelation of truths about God, seeing that God is unlike and greater than anything else that there is in the whole of existence.

Notes

1. See chap. 5, 'Religion' p. 78, above
2. Romans 1:20
3. I Kings 4:31
4. Ibid. 3:12
5. Cf. John 21:25
6. *Modern Study of the O.T. and Inspiration* (Cambridge University Press, 1909), pp. 55-6, cited by MacDonald, H.D., *Theories of Revelation* (London, Allen & Unwin, 1963), p. 237. It is only fair to add that Sprott had just referred to inspiration as enabling men 'to apprehend the Divine revelation'.
7. 'Does Christianity Need a Revelation?', *Theology*, vol. 83,

1980, pp. 109-14
  8. Isaiah 10:5 ff.
  9. Isaiah 10:24 ff.
  10. I Corinthians 1:21
  11. Job 12:2
  12. Ecclesiastes 1:18
  13. *He Came Down From Heaven* (London, Faber, 1950), p. 45
  14. *Nature, Man and God* (London, Macmillan, 1934), p. 322
  15. John 1:18

Conclusion

It has not, of course, been the purpose of this essay to deny the existence and immense importance of continuity, or to suggest that we live in a world of chaos. Obviously we do not; and, equally obviously, it is well for us that we do not. Most of our lives as individuals are 'continuous', governed by the laws of our nature and of the nature that surrounds us. We do not have to take conscious decisions to breathe or digest or circulate our blood, to blink our eyes or swallow our food, and life would be unliveable if we did have to. Indeed, most of our normal activity is more or less automatic; 'intervention' by the conscious part of our minds is needed only to spark a process off, and not all processes at that. A decision to go to the grocer's may be all the discontinuity that is required in a long and complicated process of leaving the house, shutting the door, walking along the street, avoiding collisions on the way, and so on; and the decision itself requires preceding conditions that are part of nature's continuity. I will not say that our occasional conscious judgments and decisions are taken against a background of continuity for 'background' would be the wrong word. The two are bound together; the occasional discontinuities presuppose a state of affairs to work on which is produced by natural law, and they are themselves followed by events which conform to such law.

Nor is it so very different with the action of God. So far as we can see, the vast majority of events in His universe are governed by law. 'He has made them fast for ever and ever; he has given them a law which shall not be broken.'[1] The laws may be in part statistical rather than absolute, but they are still laws:

fire and hail, snow and ice, wind and storm fulfil His word. This really *is* the background of our lives, and by its regularity we are able to exist, and think, and plan – and, it may be, worship in thanks the Lord who made it.

Yet we are not merely a part of nature, like neutrons or stars; nor merely a part of living nature, like butterflies and grass. We are people, free and conscious agents, able to reason and judge, to do good and to sin. We are constantly introducing novelty, even creativity, into our own lives, and through them into nature and the lives of others. And Christians have normally believed – rightly, to my mind – that God does the same. He is both the one who dwells in the high and holy place and the one who lives with each who is of a contrite and humble spirit. He is one who lives and loves and acts on that love, revealing, guiding, listening, answering and saving. He introduces, as we do on our lesser scale, new things into the old, things whose consequences become old and natural in their turn and may be mistakenly supposed to have no novelty behind them.

The cases are not of course exactly parallel. We are not God, – His image and likeness, maybe, – but no more. We do not create nature; He does. Our continuities are given to us by Him (as indeed is our power to introduce our discontinuities in among them). We are almost passive in the routines of our existence, carried naturally along unless the creative and conscious part of us takes action. But no-one and nothing carries God along; rather, He carries and sustains all things by the word of His power, and nothing can come or continue to exist save by His creativeness. The difference between 'nature' and 'miracle' lies not in degree of independence of God, but in what he chooses to create: continuity or discontinuity, regularity or novelty. It is only from our earthly point of view that we can speak – that I have been speaking – of His 'intervening'. Most of His world we experience as if it were autonomous; if a world could exist without God's continuing guidance, it would (we feel) be like this, regular and impersonal. But some we experience as if it were what in truth it all is, the personal activity of a God and Father.

Such novelty, such personal acts, there must be. Unless God acts in His world, there is no meaning to history, no loving concern beyond that of a remote and self-sufficient Legislator. There is no help for any who turn to Him in prayer, no reaching out of grace to those who cry to Him out of sin. God is neither the Father of our Lord Jesus Christ nor the Father of His people. The truth must of course be faced, whether it offer us comfort or no, that all this may perhaps be true; but to call it Christian is most certainly false. And to allow ourselves belief in this – an Almighty who does nothing new, an All-knowing who keeps his knowledge secret – we have to suppose that He has imposed laws and restrictions on Himself which He does not impose on us; that He gives us a freedom of action which He is Himself denied; that He is, in short, not more alive and active than us His creatures, but less.

Or we may revise our estimate of the nature of mankind. We may, wrong-headedly, deny that men and women have freedom of choice, the use of reason, or the ability to discern right and wrong, and suppose that even their awareness of the world is pointless and ineffectual. Such a race of fleshly automata might well be made in the image and likeness of the God of modern deism. But if we are unwilling to banish humanity from the world, we shall find that Deity will not be banished either.

Notes

1. Psalm 148:6